T0157404

ATHEIST IN A FOXHOLE:
One Man's Quest for Meaning

ATHEIST IN A FOXHOLE:
One Man's Quest for Meaning

Reflections, Insights, and Legacy
of Richard Alan Langhinrichs
(1921–1990)

RUTH IMLER LANGHINRICHS, *Editor*

Roberta Kreicker, Betty Casbeer Carroll,
and Jenna Gervasi-Shelly, Associate Editors

ATHEIST IN A FOXHOLE: ONE MAN'S QUEST FOR MEANING REFLECTIONS, INSIGHTS, AND LEGACY OF RICHARD ALAN LANGHINRICHS (1921–1990)

iUniverse books may be ordered through booksellers or by contacting:

iUniverse
1663 Liberty Drive
Bloomington, IN 47403
www.iuniverse.com
1-800-Authors (1-800-288-4677)

ISBN: 978-1-4917-6620-0 (sc)
ISBN: 978-1-4917-6621-7 (e)

Library of Congress Control Number: 2015906124

Print information available on the last page.

iUniverse rev. date: 05/21/2015

Contents

Part I: One Man's Journey

Part II: One Man's Legacy

List of Photos

#1: Dick and war buddy
#2: Dick and Ruth's wedding
#3: Dick, Ruth and Lucky
#4: Dick and granddaughter Sara
#5: Dick at his desk
#6: Charles Redd of Urban League
#7: Dick at three years
#8: Dick flirting with the camera
#9: Dick and Blacky
#10: Dick at eighteen
#11: Dick with his Aunt Florence and Ivan Lebamoff
#12: Ruth and daughters at Harvard 1963
#13: Julie and Jenny 1963
#14: UU Sanctuary in 1968
#15: Dick and Ruth at Easter
#16: Unitarian Universalist Meetinghouse in Fort Wayne
#17: Father's Day 1968
#18: Dick and Ruth at his desk
#19: Ruth with journal
#20: Family Portrait 1975
#21: Julie's wedding 1984
#22: David Neal's wedding
#23: Annual Retreat at Pietz Cottage
#24: Dick and Ruth with daughter Jenny
#25: Dick and Ruth with Rev. Shermie Schafer

Prologue

Dick Langhinrichs believed that saying *Yes* to the demands of life, from others, from oneself does not—in fact, should not—come easily. He felt that commitments can only be valued to the degree to which they are honored, and should not be made or taken lightly. Perhaps that is why he did not reach the decision to enter the ministry until he was forty years old, in spite of being urged by others to do so when he was seventeen.

Dick's journal entries in those interim years reveal that he was always searching for meaning, for affirmation. Finally, at midlife, he faced the dilemma of having a void, a missing sense of purpose, in spite of enjoying a successful business career, being a responsible, loving husband and father of two daughters, and having the deep respect of many.

Summoning his personal courage, and with the daring support of his family, Dick Langhinrichs, et al., pulled up roots and entered an entirely different lifestyle and role. Risks were taken, challenges were met—and ultimately Dick said *Yes* and discovered the meaning of his life.

Dick did not sail a straight course through life. He set out to write a novel and act on the New York stage. He wound up doing something far more important, building a liberal religious community in Northeastern Indiana. Along the way, he was overtaken by major global events and personal crisis. And, what happened to him—what he experienced and endured before and after his arrival in Fort Wayne—is what made his life and his ministry so rich, honest and meaningful. Both the diversity and intensity of his life experiences are what made his ministry so unique and inspiring; what caused many people to routinely commute over a hundred miles every Sunday to hear his message; what caused him to be sought for and participate in controversial leadership positions and often unpopular issues of his day.

Dick was born and raised in the rough industrial river town of Rock Island, Illinois, by an Irish Catholic mother and a German Protestant father. He learned early the meaning of dichotomy and of social injustice and suffering in the depression-wracked, wide-open streets of Rock Island, Illinois.

As a teenager, Dick became a leader in the local YMCA youth program. This provided a preview of his leadership skills, personal commitment and conviction that would often be later displayed in his adult pursuits. In the very depths of the depression, he obtained the use of an open stake-bed truck for the summer—then obtained enough contributions to permit a full truckload of boys to take a trip east to see Washington, D.C., Valley Forge, Gettysburg, Philadelphia, and other historic sites. Amazingly, while others were heading to California with all their possessions in a truck, Dick and his crew, who had worked to help pay their expenses, were off to the east coast for a cultural and camping adventure.

As Dick completed his degree at Northwestern University, World War II broke out. He became an officer in the U.S. Marine Corps after extremely rugged training at Quantico, Virginia, during a harsh winter. He was immediately deployed to combat in the South Pacific. Dick rose to the rank of lieutenant while leading his troops through the most harrowing and bloody island assault campaigns of World War II, including Saipan. As he later confided to other veterans, virtually nothing else mattered then but the success and survival of his company in combat. Men died in his arms, pinned down by enemy fire, waiting for reinforcements and for medical attention which did not come. Incredibly, Dick survived, with a Purple Heart and was awarded the Bronze Star in recognition of his heroism and leadership.

Returning to civilian life with enthusiasm and confidence, Dick headed for New York City and a stage career. While working on a novel and waiting for his big stage break, Dick established himself as a successful property manager.

His remarkable career as minister of the Fort Wayne Unitarian Universalist Congregation (UUCFW), where he served for 25 years, is documented in this book. Dick died on July 31, 1990; his memorial service can be found in the epilogue, and the books that influenced Dick's life and ministry are listed as *Sacred* Texts at the end of Part I: One Man's Journey.

—Roberta Kreicker

Preface

We'd never been a team in the conventional sense of a minister-and-his-wife team. I do not play the piano and no choir has ever begged me to sing with them. Happily, I was encouraged by the members of our church, the Unitarian Universalist Congregation of Fort Wayne, Indiana, to do my own thing. My things have tended to be an occasional religious education (RE) stint, a craft project, a social event, a summer service on Louisa May Alcott, a favorite nineteenth century woman; or May Sarton, a favorite twentieth century woman; and so on.

I think the principal reason we worked together so well—and enjoyed doing so —is that we shared a lifetime of going to the theatre together. Although we had both graduated from Northwestern University, we didn't meet until mutual best friends introduced us. The time was after World War II, and the place was New York City, where I had gone in the search of fame and fortune; and Dick had gone to write a novel, planning to live on his veteran's benefits and a part-time job. I sold my soul to Cowles Publishing Company, by working for *Look* magazine, but Dick wrote his novel and starved. But that is another story.

While we were in New York, we saw new plays by Eugene O'Neill, Tennessee Williams, and Arthur Miller. Dick and I were in the audience of every major play and a host of minor ones. The same can be said for all the time we lived in Fort Wayne. We both loved theatre. As a matter of fact, Dick majored in theatre at Northwestern's School of Speech and was nominated best director of the year for his production of *Boy Meets Girl*. We even collaborated on a theatrical production of our own, *A Night on Walden Pond* which, therefore, was a familiar joint effort in some ways and new in others. For instance, when the First Act needed to be cut Dick and I spent hours together removing words, sentences and paragraphs; each defending his or her suggestion. And yes, we were still speaking to each other afterwards, and surprisingly, talked about (perhaps) staging another script together.

Of course, theatre was only a tiny portion of our shared interests and not the most important one. After our marriage, our mutual, major goal became the establishment of a secure home for ourselves and our two daughters, Julie and Jenny.

I don't regret that I accepted the invitation from Dick (on our first date) to attend the New School of Social Research in New York City to hear Albert Camus speak on existentialism, a lecture totally in French. Dick, however, proficient in French, explained it afterward most eloquently!

I do regret that you, the reader, weren't at the Election Day party I threw at my apartment on 106 Waverly Place, a Greenwich Village fifth floor walk-up when the tide turned and Truman defeated Dewey, with Dick at the piano playing the *Missouri Waltz* over and over again, faster and faster each time as the guests tore off the black-crepe streamer arm-bands I had distributed earlier because Dewey was predicted to win.

Richard Alan Langhinrichs was an extraordinary gifted man: a man of contemplation, action, and personal charm.

I do regret that Dick is not here to re-read what he's written and what we've written about him and his life story—to tighten my sentences, to question an assertion, and ultimately to ask: whatever took you so long?

I also regret that Roberta Kreicker who solicited and assembled most of the materials is not here to see how carefully we have followed her guidelines and organization and to hear again how very grateful I am to her for her tireless efforts in visioning and sustaining this endeavor.

—Ruth Imler Langhinrichs

Introduction

The first words I wrote, as I began this book, were of our responsibility to be true to Dick's work, for it is Dick Langhinrichs who is the real messenger. This is truly Dick's legacy, his gift.

We simply packaged it. It has been a unique privilege to do so. The treasures found in the legacy of Dick's life and his work is deep and rich. Only a miniscule portion can be presented here, a harsh fact we deeply regret.

The sheer volume of Dick's ministerial work alone is encyclopedic. More than a thousand sermons were prepared and delivered by him between 1962 and 1989. Most sermons during the 1980's were taped and needed to be transcribed. In addition, the Historical Records Committee maintained a complete record of services from Dick's ordination in Fort Wayne in 1965 through his retirement in 1989. Further file searches uncovered sermons he delivered as assistant minister in Cambridge, Massachusetts, during his years at Harvard Divinity School (1962–64). All in all, a comprehensive record of Dick's work was researched in preparation for *Part I: One Man's Journey.*

Stringent selection and editorial criteria were inevitable: who could hold a book the size of four large file cabinets? The constraints of space and practicality limited the selection of only twenty-six excerpts and readings from his sermons for inclusion in this volume. An attempt to present a larger number would have prohibited doing justice to the core of their meaning; to have presented fewer would have prevented a sufficient depiction of the scope and variety of Dick's topics and concerns.

Our criteria eliminated all those with a time-bound reference (from *Montgomery to Selma* and *A Tribute to John Lennon.*) For example, sociopolitical themes were omitted, as well as services for traditional religious holidays. Rather, sermons offering individuals hope and encouragement, and those that were educational regarding Unitarian Universalism were favored. Admittedly, other considerations being equal, files containing the most complete and legible notes were chosen for their manageability. Lastly, we searched for recurring themes, for continuity. The reader will note that excerpts are not in chronological order; rather, they have been ordered by thematic content for continuity and message flow.

Packaging the biographical section, *Part II: One Man's Legacy*, was no less an intricate task. How does one edit a man's intensely engaged and engaging life?

Here, again, the task could not be measured by the number of file cabinets, but by hearts and souls of the many people whose lives Dick touched, who came forth with a wealth of warm, loving stories, fond recollections and revelations of his awe-inspiring effect on their lives.

These vignettes are expressed in the heart and soul and spirit of this volume. While, painfully, not all could be included, their essence remains deep within the lines, between these covers. What may have gone unprinted did not, in fact, go unfelt.

One brief style note is in order: throughout this volume, Dick's own words have been gleaned, not only from sermon records, but from correspondence and personal journals, as well.

We humbly acknowledge that others might make different decisions in the selections and their presentation here as William James said, "Other sculptors, other statues from the same stone!"

Nevertheless, we present this book in the image of a small door to Dick's study, opening to the reader a glimpse of his readings, his writings, his counseling and his ceremonies.

The door to Dick's study at the Unitarian Universalist meetinghouse in Fort Wayne, Indiana, bore a special greeting which we also bid you as you proceed through these portals: "Peace to All Who Enter Here".

—Roberta Kreicker, May 15, 1992

Postscript: Two decades have passed since this manuscript was initially completed. Somewhere along the way, the process stalled, and the manuscript remained unpublished. In 2012, I heard of this project and offered to get the book to market. Publishing has changed radically since 1992 with the advent of e-Readers and Print-on-Demand (POD).

Since I self-published three books myself several years ago with iUniverse.com, I felt confident I could bring the project started so long ago to fruition.

—Betty Casbeer Carroll, 2015

Atheist in a Foxhole

"They say there are no atheists in a foxhole; well, here's one!" Dick Langhinrichs frequently joked this way with his fellow Marines during World War II, concealing his intense search for a meaningful relationship with God.

Dick's search is illustrated by his writings in a battered stationery packet, emblazoned *United States Marine Corps*, which he carried and preserved as best he could, throughout the South Pacific. The worn and stained (coffee? mud? blood?) brittle yellow parchment folder contains a dozen or so pages of small handwriting on both sides, evidence that space, as well as time, was at a premium on the battleground.

His written musings contain this entry, reflecting a search for some blessed state and his certainty of its nonexistence:

> Now it comes clear to me. I have instinctively craved the peaceful fullness of a broadly human, deep-rooted, traditionally accepted belief and its expression in the material forms of the world. I have so hankered after such a protective cloak that I have wildly, quixotically sought to find such an element in the mercantile life of Midwestern United States. I have forced myself to find solace in YMCA campfires and Marine Corps traditions, while blindly searching on and on for a key that would open the passageway to a blessed state that is nonexistent.

In the following passage, Dick, a twenty-two year old Marine assigned to combat, ruminated on his slow maturity and attempted to understand the duality-conflicts in his mind:

> My maturity comes and comes slowly. Only today did I discover and really know that education consists in assimilating and learning by rote many statements and beliefs represented to be factual and then, painfully absorbing those representations into one's personality.
>
> The selection of truth; of important writing; the understanding of music and poetry and art; the awareness of life as it appears in my mind is a painful process of assimilation that cannot be controlled or directed beyond making some basic choices that are essentially accidental in their very existence. The rest is intuitive and guided by heredity and environment which were totally beyond my control.
>
> My mind is principally a duality: passion and morality. Reason, which might temper it and give it a triangular structure, is powerless in the face of intuitive desire. Reason fails utterly as a moderator and usually seeks recourse by aligning itself with my Puritan morality, leaving me despondent over my inability to act as my whole being dictates it should. The conflict is particularly violent, since my morality is dictatorial.

World War II broke out as Dick completed his undergraduate degree at the Northwestern University School of Speech, in Evanston, Illinois.

In 1942, Dick volunteered for the United States Marine Corps Reserves. Years later, Dick described his Marine entry interview in an informal *Odyssey* account shared with ministerial colleagues [Ohio Valley Unitarian Universalist Ministers' Association chapter meeting, December 8, 1986]:

> Pearl Harbor Day was during my senior year at Northwestern. At that time, while there was a draft, people were not registered for the draft until they were twenty-one years of age. I was not to be twenty-one for yet another year. I had no reason to have to go into the service, and I didn't immediately respond to all the pressure and instant patriotism, but I did eventually volunteer.

Because of my perceptions of social snobbery in college, I did not want to be an officer. I insisted on being an enlisted man, which I thought would be much more democratic.

They waited and waited to call me up. Finally, although I was slightly underweight at 135 pounds but passed all other examinations with flying colors, I was called in by an officer who, behind closed doors and with tears streaming down his cheeks, demanded, "Why are you insisting on being an enlisted man?"

I replied that I believed in democracy and that there were a lot of questions about *elitism* in the officer corps and I didn't think I would fit in there, that I wouldn't feel comfortable about it.

The officer said he had just received news that his best friend had been killed at Guadalcanal and that many others of his friends who were officers were being killed in the South Pacific; that the enemy was killing second lieutenants faster than the U.S. could train them.

He told me that I had a patriotic duty to train as a second lieutenant, rather than go in as a private. Believe it or not, I bought it hook, line, and sinker. Death had a great attraction, and that's been a recurrent theme of my life.

Dick's first assignment as a machine gun platoon leader of Company K, Third Battalion, Sixth Marine Regiment, was in New Zealand, in preparation for the invasions of the Marianas Islands.

Dick was in the first wave to land at Saipan Island on June 6, 1944 [D-Day in Europe]. The invasion began with 253 enlisted men and nine officers; at the end of six days, there were 37 enlisted men and one officer, Dick.

When these extremely severe casualties necessitated it, Dick acted both as company executive officer and commander at Saipan and Tinian.

Lew Weber, an eighteen-year-old private first class at the time of the Saipan invasion, recalls: "Dick was the only officer who was not wounded or killed. He took command of our company and did a great job. Langhinrichs was a brave officer. He never let up on his responsibilities."

E. L. Fritz was on board the same amphibious tank with Dick the morning of that invasion. Although Fritz was a corporal and two years younger than Dick, he was considered to be a *veteran* having been in the invasions of Guadalcanal and Tarawa. Fritz relates that he and Dick had a brief private conversation about the coming invasion and that Langhinrichs was anxious about going into his first battle as a young inexperienced officer, and expressed concern about handling himself in battle. I told him that we all were a team and that most of us had enough experience that we would just perform as if it were maneuvers, and that he would be just like the rest of us—some scared, some aggressive, some careful—but brave enough to do the job. He was as much a man as any of us.

One of Dick's close friends, a retired Marine colonel, Graham H. Kreicker [former member of the Unitarian Universalist Congregation of Fort Wayne], shares the following from conversations with Dick:

> Just twenty-three years old and holding the rank of second lieutenant, Dick led his troops through the most harrowing and bloody island assault campaigns of the war, including Saipan. While pinned down by enemy fire, waiting for reinforcements and for medical attention which did not come, men literally died in his arms. As he later confided to other veterans, virtually nothing else mattered then but the success and survival of his company in combat.

Incredibly, Dick survived, with a Purple Heart; he was also awarded the Bronze Star in recognition of his heroism and leadership at Saipan. Not surprisingly, Dick's "Marine Corps writing packet" contains only one war-related incident:

> When we went on the Rabbit Hunt on Saipan, a mortar platoon flushed a Japanese family from a cave. The mother and daughter gave themselves up, but the father took to his heels. One of the men shot the father with a pistol. The man was wounded twice in the extreme left chest; he fell to the ground, twitching like a slaughtered chicken. A corporal walked up, looked at him and said, "This'll put him out of his misery," then fired five rounds from an M-1 into his head, blowing it off: Murder?

Dick rarely spoke of his traumatic war experiences, but he did share these vivid recollections more than four decades later:

> Near the end of the invasion, Louie, a young man from Peoria, Illinois, and a key person in my platoon, was severely wounded by a grenade on the second day that we were on Saipan. All officers, at that time, were equipped with morphine needles and had been carefully instructed that, if there was to be with certainty a kind of heavily bleeding wound, we were not to use these needles because morphine would cause or hasten death. There were only certain circumstances under which we were to use morphine.
>
> Louie was in agonizing pain, screaming and begging for morphine, but he had the kind of wound that prohibited the use of morphine. This went on for about an hour. I did not give him the morphine and still, to this day, I have nightmares about that decision. I know that if I had given him the morphine, he would have died— which he did anyhow. I can still hear him screaming. In Saipan, a couple of unusual things happened. My platoon captured the first Japanese civilians that had been taken captive during the war. This was three years into World War II. The policy of the U.S. government, when at all possible, was to kill all Japanese and not take any captives.
>
> There were so many that it didn't warrant taking captives, but we captured a mother and daughter in a farm house. These two people and two guys from my platoon were on the cover of *Time* magazine back in 1944.
>
> At the end of the invasion, we kept moving north on Saipan Island, which was a very rocky narrow mountain in the Pacific. The civilians there were farming sugar cane and they gradually moved closer and closer to the cliffs at the far north end of the island. When things got desperate, the Japanese families would go to the water and bathe. Then the entire family would hike to the top of the cliff where the father would pitch off the infants and small children. The teen-aged youngsters, the grandparents, the mother and, finally, the father would exterminate themselves, rather than allow capture by us. It was a case of honor and fear of what we Americans would do. There were literally hundreds of Japanese suicides in the summer of 1944.

Needless to say, this was a very shaping experience in relationship to: my religious belief, my atheism, and my convictions. This was even more intensified for me, because the next invasion I was involved in was Okinawa.

In Okinawa, the Japanese were so desperate that they began sending in kamikaze pilots, flying planes purposely into ships to sink them. The ship that I was on had a kamikaze attack. I have an indelible picture in my mind of the kamikaze pilot's face as he flew into the stacks. His expression is still vivid to me, this minute. Again, whole questions arose: What are we committed to? How do people become committed? What will we live for; what will we sacrifice; what will we do and why?"

In the late summer of 1944 at Saipan, Dick was promoted to first lieutenant and appointed adjutant of the third battalion with the job of reconstructing 1300 personnel records which had been lost or mislaid because of ships sinking. He was highly commended for his success with this task, and for his contribution to the rebuilding of morale in his badly shot-up battalion.

While at Saipan, Dick and the regimental Red Cross director organized a volunteer teaching program for men who had quit high school to join the Marines. They assisted several men in obtaining diplomas and in qualifying for post-war college work, using University of Wisconsin extension program materials.

Predictably, they also organized a literary discussion group. The motley mix of participants included, in addition to its two organizers, the Jewish chaplain, an art director for Walt Disney Studios, an English professor, and a mysterious man who turned out later to be a professional Communist Party organizer.

Dick's Marine-issue writing packet is confined, for the most part, to character sketches for the novel he hoped to write after the war, personal book review notes, and a brief reading list notably including Emery Reves' *The Anatomy of Peace* and Franz Werfel's *Embezzled Heaven*. These, and the remainder of books appearing on Dick's World War II reading list, are indicated with an asterisk (*) in the *Sacred* Texts (at the end of Part I).

Only a few inner reflections appear in this packet. Among them are these reactions to the premature news of war's end, written in Okinawa where Dick was serving as battalion adjutant. Feelings on the evening of August 10 and the morning of August 11, 1945:

> The news of Japan's offer to accept the Potsdam proposals, but keep Hirohito, came in about 10:15 last evening. Excitement spread through camp carrying a false message with shouts of "the war is over." At midnight, I heard the correct information. The officers on duty here today all resent the apparent dissatisfaction of the American public with the terms, and hope the government will accept them. I rather agree with them, but am not wholly convinced.

> My personal reaction last night was mixed elation and an indescribable dread. I thought immediately. Well, this is now the post-war world. I am so very afraid of the future and have been since my early college days. After entering the service, this attitude has intensified to a point, particularly unpleasant, just after being placed here. I seem to want the security of a job and income that life gives me, if any: such a fool.

Dick related to associates that, throughout the war, he did not return to the religion of his youth. He held to his claim of being *an atheist in a foxhole*, would not give in, and didn't go to the chaplain for help. Dick said that he argued with the chaplain about religion and the best seller, by Lloyd C. Douglas, *The Robe*. In Dick's words:

> Half the guys in my battalion were reading it and they thought it was the most wonderful book they had ever read. It was about the life of Jesus and his robe, and the magical effect his robe had on people after the crucifixion. I thought it was just plain bullshit. I'd tell them, this discussion could go on all day and all night and it did.

In his twenties, Dick struggled for an integration of his inner conflicts which he identified as a duality of passion and morality; his search for self, meaning and God came hard. It may never have come easy. However, his atheistic protests failed to convince at least one of his comrades, who assured him that he had a deep abiding faith that would emerge one day.

Those assurances were prophetic—as Dick's remarks, made in retrospect more than two decades later from Fort Wayne, Indiana's Unitarian Universalist pulpit, indicate:

> I had, in the Marine Corps, come to recognize that the superstitious god of Christianity is not what religion is all about. But I didn't know quite what to put in its place.
>
> I had the awful experience of having many, many colleagues and friends killed, some very close to me. The master sergeant of my company was hit by a bazooka shell from a Japanese tank. His head was blown off. He was only an arm's length from me and all I got were two little pieces of shrapnel, one in my arm and one in my ear. Eight other people, who were standing just as close, were also killed.
>
> I came to believe that life is indeed very, very valuable. But believing in God is not what keeps you from getting killed in wars. And it's not what keeps bad things from happening to you. What I gradually learned in the Marine Corps has come to be my deepest conviction—that we need a religion of spirituality, not of superstition.

However, at war's end, Dick was still searching and, in his self-evaluation, he was a psychological basket case and a hero without affirmation. His quest for serenity and meaning continued.

Part I

One Man's Journey

Searching for Connection

None but the Lonely Heart
Spreading Sacrifice Equitably
Truly Amazing Grace
To Seek the Truth

Burb Whipple and Dick Langhinrichs at Saipan in 1944

None but the Lonely Heart

A report of a National Institute of Mental Health Conference in 1982, *Preventing the Harmful Consequences of Severe and Persistent Loneliness*, is, I believe, the first in the history of the mental health profession explicitly focused on the phenomenon of extensive loneliness in our culture. Here are some extracts from the preface to that writing:

> Loneliness: The word evokes two distinct responses from professionals and lay people. Some dismiss loneliness as a petty nuisance which, like the common cold, is nothing to take too seriously. Others view loneliness as a major disturbance associated with intense feelings of isolation and a profound sense of having no one who cares or understands. Actually, loneliness takes both of these forms.
>
> Transient feelings of loneliness are both common and relatively harmless. Most people overcome occasional bouts of loneliness quickly and without assistance. In contrast, severe and persistent loneliness is an extremely painful experience that undermines psychological well-being and is a significant risk factor in psychological dysfunction and mental disorder.

Several clinicians have called attention to the significance of loneliness for mental health. Harry Stack Sullivan [American psychiatrist, 1892–1949] defined loneliness as the powerful response experienced when the basic human need for interpersonal intimacy is not fulfilled. He argued that loneliness is a more powerful motivator than anxiety. Frieda Fromm-Reichmann [German psychoanalyst who later became a naturalized American citizen, 1839–1957] suggested that extreme loneliness renders people emotionally paralyzed and helpless. If allowed to persist, loneliness

5

leads ultimately to the development of psychotic states. Robert S. Weiss [American sociologist and educator, born 1925] characterized loneliness as annoying distress without redeeming features. Although loneliness has some similarity to such related states as depression or grief, Weiss emphasized that loneliness is a distinct form of distress worthy of attention in its own right.

Research focused on social support has demonstrated that personal relationships are crucial to psychological well-being and can provide a buffer against the negative effects of life's stress.

Recent studies [1985] focusing specifically on loneliness have shown that loneliness is a pervasive problem. It has been estimated that one American in four has experienced loneliness in the past few weeks: perhaps as much as 10 percent of the population of the United States suffers from severe and persistent loneliness.

The significance of these figures is highlighted by evidence linking loneliness to depression, suicide, delinquency, alcohol abuse and other mental health problems. Loneliness is a warning signal.

We live in between-ness, in between festivals of gratitude and joy, in between seasons of contrasting color, in between floods of brightness and seas of whiteness. We live in between-ness, on a remote island outpost in a fathomless space. Between stars and moons and planets and void; surrounded by meteors, comets, rays, nothingness, in which there is no right or left, no up or down, only between-ness.

We live in between-ness, walking from city of birth to death, hoping along the way to see something of beauty, to touch hands with those we love, to give more than we get, to make some sense of it all. We live in between-ness.

The National Institute of Mental Health is working to provide an additional category of loneliness, as a recognizable human condition that either is directly or indirectly involved with the development of more serious mental health problems. Sometimes loneliness is so chronic that it has already become a mental health problem in and of itself.

Following the earlier works of Harry Stack Sullivan and Frieda Fromm-Reichmann, our Unitarian Universalist publishing house, Beacon Press, published *Pursuit of Loneliness* (1970) by Philip Slater, the American sociologist and author.

Despite all of these efforts from diverse sources and people, loneliness has continued to be regarded as a situation somewhat akin to the common cold—everybody gets them and most everybody lives through them and we shouldn't take them very seriously.

What things would help, what things should we do? In the analysis of the initial stage of loneliness—a separation of personal, temporary crisis—can be made from cultural loneliness. The personal forms of loneliness have to do with relatedness. At its extreme form, it is the death of a parent, or spouse, a loved one, a person with whom one has been involved in a very intimate connection and developed mutuality and sharing that is suddenly taken away. That disruption can either temporarily or permanently affect how we relate to people in the future.

Other kinds of personal disruption are events like moving to a different community, or going off to college in a strange community. It's almost universal that students in their freshman year are severely lonely.

A supplemental way of characterizing loneliness is to consider its cultural aspects. This would include the contributions to loneliness of the increase of two parents working, for example, or single-parent families. When there is much less present and visible interchange between children and adults, what effect does that have on children growing up in our society? In *Pursuit of Loneliness*, Philip Slater identifies the cultural aspects of loneliness as being an inevitable characteristic of the culture and society in which we live. Slater finds that the things we are most deeply committed to are in economic and social realms, and inevitably going to create great loneliness. And furthermore, there are three human desires that are deeply and uniquely frustrated by the American culture today. The first is our human desire for community, the wish to live in trust and cooperation with one's fellows in a total and visible collective entity.

The second is the desire for engagement, the wish to come directly to grips with social and interpersonal problems and to confront on equal terms an environment which is not composed of ego extension. And the third is the desire for dependence. This is one that, in my experience, most people favor to deny. In response to personal crisis in our culture, I think we are trained from infancy on to develop, as rapidly as we can the means of handling crisis alone. To do so proves how stable a human being you are. It proves how sound you are with your mental health; it proves how resourceful you are if you handle something all by yourself—and never let others recognize that you are hurting. Our culture is built on the independence of individuals and the responsibility of individuals to take care of themselves.

In addition, I think that we are raised in a culture—but this is not peculiar to us, though it seems to be more intense in our American culture than anywhere else—in which nobody should be dependent on anybody for anything. That's part of becoming an adult. It isn't just in time of crisis, but it's throughout one's personal life and lifestyle.

I think Slater is making a point that we need to consider when we attempt to get serious about loneliness and what we might do about it. Certainly, there could be many things we could change in our culture to reduce the amount of separation and loneliness and lack of interrelatedness. For instance, some issues to consider are: the suburban migration or our *vigilante* attitude where everybody is armed, certainly a self-defeating kind of behavior. Can we ameliorate loneliness within our present cultural setting?

Or are we, as Slater contended years ago and some mental health professionals contended even earlier, confronted with the necessity of modifying at least our cultural system and cultural expectations? If you're feeling deprived, go buy yourself something, our culture declares. Spend some money. That will make you joyous. How long that joy will last, actually, is questionable. But we all buy into it!

Slater, in his conclusion, has a section entitled *Alone Together.* He says the most serious internal danger to establishing a new culture is the insidious transmission of individualism from the old culture to the present one, in part through the confusion of *individualism* with an otherwise healthy emphasis on emotional expression. Ambivalence about the issue of individualism versus social commitment is deep in our country.

Anarchy is merely a radical extension of what we presently do. It's a way of retaining the pristine American fantasy of being special, a condition which America both promises and withholds, more than any other society in history. The unstated rider to "do your own thing", however, is that if and when you do, everybody will watch you and you'll become an instant celebrity! But in the satisfying society, this specialness is not needed.

For a satisfying society to exist, the recognition that people can and must make demands upon one another must also exist.

Ironically, what we've done in the last twenty years, starting with the movements for *intimacy* sessions and so on, is generate a *loneliness industry.* There are all kinds of commercial solutions to loneliness: you can go to group therapy, to a retreat, to a singles club, to a dating service, or even to a church event! Much of this activity is very commercially staged to trade on the widespread loneliness in our culture—but most of these things don't help very much. Ultimately, all of the *do it yourself* movements, inviting as they may be, have a way, if we get into them very deeply, of intensifying our feelings of loneliness.

Finally, this story from *Unifiers,* a meditation book from the San Diego UU church *Oops,* by Tom Oentough: "I want to thank you, Mr. Marx, for all the enjoyment you've given the world," said a friendly pastor when he was introduced to Groucho Marx. To which Groucho replied, "And I want to thank you for all the enjoyment you've taken out of it."

There was a rule, believe it or not, back in the early days of the sunday school movement in the late 19th Century which read: "Do not attend Sunday School to have fun. You're not there to enjoy yourself." Times have changed. Thankfully, religious community is the place where we can both give and receive deep, enduring enjoyment that can alleviate loneliness.

Related Reading

Prayer is the very soul and essence of religion... but prayer is not asking. It is a longing of the soul... a daily admission of one's weakness and an attempt to prepare ourselves to share the sufferings of our fellows whoever they may be.

**—Mohandas K. Gandhi, Indian political,
spiritual leader and lawyer, 1869–1948**

Dick and Ruth's wedding, 1959

*Ruth's dog Lucky Starlight assesses his
new home and master, Dick.*

Spreading Sacrifices Equitably

Sharing inevitable sacrifices equitably is an ideal which many societies have been called upon to meet throughout human history. Rarely, if ever, have we or our ancestors responded with grace. What role might religion play to make such sharing somewhat more equitable?

I thought long and hard about times when a nation or a society or a group of people we could identify as a culture banded together to make an effort—with at least a degree of success—to share sacrifices equitably. Those that I could bring to mind all had connections with war.

There are some occasions when a nation or group of people faced with a foe do gather together, marshal their resources, energize their political processes in ways that even out the kind of sharing that goes on among people: at least to a considerable degree—to a much higher degree than is normal—within those countries.

In this sense, I think that is what happened in the United States for the first couple of years after World War II's Pearl Harbor. I think that American citizens generally were prepared to sacrifice a good deal in the way of personal expectations, lifestyles and career goals to meet the needs of the hour. This willingness to sacrifice began to play itself out before the war was over; and it certainly did not last to any significant degree in the period after the war.

You may not agree with my illustration, but I have some sense that there was a time between 1941 and 1943 or 1944 when there was some genuine sharing of goals and expectations and a willingness on the part of many, perhaps most, people in our society, in our nation, to do whatever needed to be done and to make their contribution equitably.

We've all been in smaller groups where, in an effort to get an activity off the ground we've succeeded in energizing people around a cause, around a goal, around an expectation. Occasionally we see this happen in the political process.

An American writer on political and social issues, David Halberstam, concludes in his book *The Reckoning* (1986) on a sobering note:

> No country, including America, is likely ever to be as rich as America had been from 1945 to 1975, and other nations were following the Japanese into middle-class existence, which meant that life for most Americans was bound to become leaner, but in the middle of 1936, there seemed little awareness of this, let alone concern about it. Few were discussing how best to adjust the nation to an age of somewhat diminished expectations, or how to marshal its abundant resources for survival in a harsh, unforgiving new world, or how to spread the inevitable sacrifices equitably.

The Apostle Paul pointed out that a body of church members are all interrelated, interconnected in significant ways. I think that what we need to be doing in the United States today is getting much more information to each other and recognizing that we need to find ways to cooperate. Yes, to compete—in the sense of competing against ourselves, to do the best possible job that we can—but to do this through cooperation rather than destructive kinds of competition. Most of all, our efforts need to be under girded with excellence. Such efforts are religious, spiritual qualities as much as they are political or social.

It seems to me that we do face difficult times. They may not prove to be as difficult, as seemingly hopeless, as some people writing about the situation today would have us believe, but it's very clear that our priorities are not set in a very stable, significant way when we're asked repeatedly to choose politicians on the basis of whether they are optimists or pessimists. We don't want any prophets of doom or gloom to be elected—which is another way of saying we don't want anybody who is going to talk about the realities of the situation we're in.

If we don't want to hear the truth and we don't want to do anything about it, we've made a choice. And it seems to me, much of the time, we do not want to hear the truth about ourselves. The time has come for us to face up to reality.

The time has come for us to seek to find ways of building new cooperation, new education, new quality into life, and to sort out those things that are really significant from the things that are not so important.

I think we all need to be prepared to help each other to face the future with open eyes and realism.

Related Reading

I have spoken of the grounds and importance of that honor or respect which is due from us, and enjoined on us, toward all human beings. Perhaps none of you have yet heard of or can comprehend the tone of voice in which a man, thoroughly impressed with this sentiment, would speak to a fellow-creature. It is a language hardly known on earth; and no eloquence, I believe, has achieved such wonders as it is destined to accomplish. The great revelation which man now needs is a revelation of man to himself. The faith which is most wanted is a faith in what we and our fellow-beings may become a faith in the divine germ or principle in every soul.

**—William Ellery Channing, American Unitarian
minister and author, 1780–1842**

Truly Amazing Grace

What is grace? M. Scott Peck, M.D. and psychiatrist, wrote about grace in *The Road Less Traveled* [1978]. Dr. Peck says that the most important factor in effective, successful work with people who have mental problems is a matter of grace. He also attributes grace to much of what goes on in the prospects of physical illness and in problems of life in general. Under the heading of *The Definition of Grace*, he describes grace as a whole variety of phenomena that have the following characteristics in common:

> They (phenomena that) serve to nurture—support, protect, and enhance—human life and spiritual growth. The mechanism of their action is either incompletely understandable (as in physical resistance and dreams) or totally obscure (as in paranormal phenomena) according to the principles of natural law as interpreted by current scientific thinking.

> Their occurrence is frequent, routine, commonplace and essentially universal among humanity. Although potentially influenced by human consciousness, their origin is outside of the conscious will and *beyond the process of conscious decision-making.*

I think the last characteristic is the most important one since Peck gives this example from an early time in his own life. Coming home from school one day, he fell on the ice into a busy street where there was a lot of snow and ice; a car skidded to a halt with the wheels almost over him, but not actually hitting him.

Peck says that this may be an illustration of grace in the sense that his subconscious told him where to fall on that ice. It may even have sent some vibes to the driver and influenced that person to come to a halt.

And that the car did come to a halt. Something synchronistic happened in that circumstance that defies explanation. Now this does not mean, obviously, that anybody can throw themselves into the street and expect cars to come to a halt.

We all share similar experiences when things turn out well for us, when we have no reason to expect that they will. We also have experiences in our lives where we expend a great amount of energy in trying to bring something to be—that we're determined must happen. It eludes us and eludes us and eludes us until sometimes, quite mysteriously, something totally unexpected occurs that alters the situation entirely and makes that thing which we most wanted to have happen impossible.

Or, the thing that we wanted and fought and worked so hard to bring about comes into being, but comes into being in ways that we had not anticipated and clearly has nothing to do with how much energy we expended on trying to bring it about.

How, then, does grace occur and what does it mean to us? In the first place, I think grace is something that occurs to us if we really allow ourselves to get in touch with our subconscious mind, with the positive healthy impulses that exist in all of us and are able to influence our activities if we allow them to do so.

Most of you are familiar with the fact that if you say to yourself, *"I really want to dream, I'm going to allow myself to dream tonight,"* you will dream even if you don't think you've ever had a dream before in your life! Apparently, that *permission* enables your subconscious to get in touch with your healthy impulses and messages.

Another way to allow grace to function in our lives is to allow ourselves to be open to life, to the reality of life, in ways that enable us to harmonize our life with reality and to cooperate with it.

To use an extreme example, if I have a broken leg, the first thing I have to do is accept the fact that my leg is in a cast. I either have to have crutches or a wheelchair. Although we do not recognize such acceptance so easily when it's emotional bandages rather than physical bandages that we're carrying about, cooperating with their reality allows grace to enter.

Recognition of the reality of what we have to accept and then to move on seeking harmonious ways, cooperative ways, creative ways, to function regardless, helps us to make the most of our potentiality.

We all can think of those who triumph over their difficulties and allow life to happen to them; who can minimize the things that are possible in life and who thrive on life; who lead a joyous existence.

And there are others, with the same set of afflictions or difficulties, who are constantly regretting and feeling angry, and resisting any adaptation to their difficulties.

People who accept their limitations and allow positive things to happen to them tend to be the people who get the most out of existence. It's no guarantee that everything, as the American musical comedy star Ethel Merman [1909–84] sings, is *going to be coming up roses*, but the feeling that Ethel Merman expresses when she sings Stephen Sondheim's *Everything's Coming Up Roses* is a sense of being in tune and harmony with life. And when one is in tune and in harmony with life, and one recognizes one's limitations as well as one's potentiality, even if there are other people who look on our lives as pretty grim, one can feel inside as if everything's coming up roses. And that's part of what grace is.

When we feel that everything's coming up roses, chances are—again, it's not guaranteed—situations will turn out better than they would have if we feel we're tromping around gradually sinking in quicksand, about to go under. And chances are that if we live our lives expecting to be engulfed in quicksand, we will probably end up suffocating in quicksand. Not inevitably. But chances are.

Another way to experience grace is to allow fortuitous circumstances from the outside to happen to us. If we are open to other people and to the events that go on in the world, the influence of positive people and positive events in the world over which we have no control may act in our lives. Give them a chance to act.

The people that least experience Grace are those people who live their lives on rigid schedules with rigid expectations of how life must be. And if it does not turn out and function to their expectations, they get angry and insist that other people have to conform to their way of doing things or else—and so limit themselves constantly regarding positive things happening from others in the world about them.

What obstructs us from grace? I think the obvious obstruction is laziness. The scientific term is entropy. The desire to leave things the way they are prevents us from mustering the energy to bring about change, or to open ourselves up to change. We often think that it is less difficult to leave things in their painful state than to invest energy to bring about change in our circumstances.

Equally important, but often overlooked, is the fear that many of us have: what if we really got our lives straightened out? Wouldn't we have so much energy and power, there's no telling what we might do? If we were really functioning at full capacity, what kind of trouble might we create out there in the world? I think it is a widespread human fear that we will create more harm than good. This fear can only stand in the way of our being willing to invest ourselves and of allowing good things to occur in our lives.

Remember, good things have happened, good things are happening, and, if we allow ourselves to be open to it, good things will continue to happen.

> Amazing grace! How sweet the sound that saved a wretch like me! I once was lost, but now am found; was blind but now I see. Twas grace that taught my heart to fear and grace my fears relieved; how precious did that grace appear the hour I first believed! Through many dangers, toils and snares, I have already come; tis grace that brought me safe thus far, and grace will lead me home.

I think this hymn's message is one that we as Unitarian Universalists have neglected; it is true for our faith, if we allow it to be true. It is grace that's brought us safe this far and grace shall lead us home, if we allow it.

And let's do allow it in the years ahead.

Related Reading

I think this is implicit in much of our thinking. Consider the man who says, 'Oh, God, I'm nothing! I'm nothing! I'm only an insignificant speck in a vast universe. I'm really nothing!' But this same man will also say: I am human, and humans are of course superior to animals (for God has privileged us by giving us free will), and animals are of course on a higher level than plants. Now, flowers are plants. But a flower! What could be more beautiful and perfect than a flower? A flower is not lacking in anything! A flower is as beautiful and perfect as it can be. It is God's creation at its best. It cannot be any better than it is. So here I am obviously better than a flower. A flower is perfect, yet I am only a miserable nothing. Is this not remarkable?

—Raymond M. Smullyan, American mathematician, logician and author of *A Strange Paradox*

To Seek the Truth

Every morning we have eyes for the new day and hold authority to establish the reality of our world. To frame the question rightly is the beginning of wisdom.

The prophet Jeremiah warned society, warned his culture, warned the leaders of his time, about the way in which they were conducting themselves:

> Go up and down the streets of Jerusalem and see for yourselves; search her wide squares: can you find any man who acts justly, who seeks the truth...but your wrongdoing has upset nature's order, and your sins have kept from you her kindly gifts. For among my people there are wicked men, who lay snares like a fowler's net and set deadly traps to catch men. Their houses are full of fraud, as a cage is full of birds. They grow rich and grand, bloated and rancorous; their thoughts are all of evil, and they refuse to do justice; the claims of the orphan they do not put right nor do they grant justice to the poor. Shall I not punish them for this, says the Lord; shall I not take vengeance on such a people?— *Jeremiah 5:1, 5:25–29 NEB*

And this from the first chapter *The Way We Are* from English historian James Burke's book, *The Day the Universe Changed*:

> Somebody once observed to the eminent Austrian philosopher Ludwig Wittgenstein [1889–1951] how stupid Medieval Europeans before the time of Copernicus [Polish astronomer 1473–1543] must have been that they could have looked at the sky and thought that the sun was circling the earth. Wittgenstein

is said to have replied, "I agree, but I wonder what it would have looked like if the sun had been circling the earth."

The point is that it would look exactly the same. Even when we observe nature, we see what we want to see. Nature is disordered, powerful, chaotic, and, through fear of the chaos, we impose a system upon it.

We need to have an overall explanation of what the universe is and how it functions. To achieve this overall view, we develop explanatory theories which will give structure to natural phenomena. We classify nature into a coherent system which appears to do what we say it does.

This view of the universe permeates all aspects of our life. All communities, in all places at all times, manifest their view of reality in what they do. The entire culture reflects the contemporary model of reality. We are what we know and when our body of knowledge changes, so do we.

Our modern view is a mixture of present knowledge and past viewpoints which have stood the test of time and, for one reason or another, remain valuable in new circumstances.

Much of contemporary science and philosophy questions the existence of, or the possibility of, absolute truth, known or to be known. As we affirm our covenant, we as Unitarian Universalists commit ourselves to seek the truth in love.

However, James Burke asks:

> But which truth? The brain imposes visual order on chaos by grouping sets of signals, rearranging them or rejecting them. Reality is what the brain makes it. To quote Wittgenstein, "You are what you want to be, you are what you want to see. All observations of the external world are therefore theory-laden."

The first people to develop Philosophy were the Greeks. The significance of this is that philosophy, as different from religion, existed nowhere else in the world. People who thought about and raised issues about the ultimate questions of life existed only in Greece.

Greek philosophers believed that there was a natural explanation for everything that existed in the world. They did not resort to magical or supernatural explanations. They believed that there were causes and effects, natural explanations for the manifestations of the physical world.

The Greeks developed and were deeply committed to a whole discipline known as logic, governing the way of thinking and the process of asking questions. The ultimate bottom line in Greek culture and its contribution to us three thousand years later is its system of thought which was a questioning system.

The Unitarian Universalist view of the universe is essentially an optimistic one because it's a kind of marriage between law and innovation. Burke insists that since we have to have a way to get along with each other: a) We must have a legal system; b) We must have a system of operating that we know as the republican system; and at the same time, c) We need to create a culture, a society in which innovation is desirable and possible.

As Jeremiah perceived in ancient Israel, it is important that truth somehow be linked to justice under law; that mercy and fairness are essential in a society. Simultaneously, a tension must exist that encourages innovation. (There is often a conflict between the rule by law and one by innovation.)

Important things have happened within the last fifty years which have raised some issues that prior human beings did not foresee. For instance, scientists in Germany, in Denmark, and elsewhere working in a coherent cooperation in the 1920s led to German physicist Werner Heisenberg's *Uncertainty Principle*.

The *Uncertainty Principle* is, on the one hand, extremely simple, and, on the other hand, extremely complex. According to this principle, the smallest form of matter that we can identify is both a particle and its wave. If you're trying to look at it as a particle, you can't see that it's a wave; but if you try to look at it as a wave, you can't see that it's a particle. You can't see both at the same time. You're always in a gray area. You're never certain of what you're looking at or how to measure it.

Scientific knowledge, therefore, is not the clearest representation of what reality is. This we have gradually and grudgingly learned. There are limits to scientific knowledge and how closely it approximates our understanding of reality.

Recalling Wittgenstein's question about how it would have looked if the sun were rotating around the earth (and his answer that there wouldn't have been any way one could tell the difference) illustrates that our *knowledge* is relative to belief. Whether the earth is turning or the sun is rising, the universe is what we say it is.

What scientists will say fifty years from now may be radically different from what they are now saying: following that logic, scientific truth, at least is relative.

The question is, does this then mean that all religion, all spirituality is relativistic also? I would suggest the possibility that, "Yes that may be the case." Indeed, religion is what human beings decide to believe that it is. And there are different positions taken by different people. There is no uniformity of belief, and there are many options that are open.

Critics from either end of the spectrum speak out. On the one hand, they argue that we can't afford this relativistic viewpoint because, with such a view, justice will never prevail and religion surely has to make a stronger, deeper demand on us. On the other hand, others argue that a religion designed to meet the present needs of the times may be totally invalid a hundred years from now. This thought alone leaves people feeling defenseless. People have a need to believe in absolute truth.

There are some positive things, of course, about accepting a relativistic view of religion, if that is necessitated by the view that we take here of science and of truth. In the first place, it means that everybody becomes responsible to a degree for what goes on in the world. It seems to me that this viewpoint neutralizes all sorts of extremism. If we, indeed, had a genuinely tolerant culture, extremism of any kind would be very difficult for people to maintain.

In a relativistic view of religion, religion becomes one of helping us to define, understand, and comprehend the relationships that exist between various facts, various pieces of information, and various structures. Such a religion becomes, then, a study of a process of evaluation rather than an accumulation of facts to be memorized. It's a technique for a style of living and surviving in the world, rather than a pouring-in process of certain facts, historic or otherwise.

To sum up, then, is there absolute truth? If so, is it accessible to us? Increasingly, the answer from the scientific world today seems to be that there is not. The world of science reports dead ends and walls that exist beyond which scientists don't feel they will ever be able to move. Their arguments often tend to be circular.

This, in turn, brings me to something I was taught to suspect in philosophy. It is a statement about God and the universe, which was delivered by St. Thomas Aquinas (1224–1274), the Italian philosopher who created philosophical systems with implications for the nature of reason, "There can't be anything else because universe means everything, so there can't be anything outside."

This is a circular argument that comes back to zero without having said anything. Sounds very impressive if you just swallow it and let it go down, but it doesn't really go all the way down.

Our question then, "Is there absolute truth?" has done much to bring us to today's world. Both its advantages and disadvantages are the result of a particular style of thought that was developed in ancient Greece and has been kept alive down to the present time. Is religious spiritual relativism desirable or inevitable? Is it avoidable, and if so, how? I think the answers to these questions are still out there waiting to be determined. In the meantime, we should take seriously the positive things being said about relativism. Meanwhile, the question is do we have the courage to live in a world that is willing to ask all of these questions? Certainly, courage will be an important component of survival.

Without fear, we can follow the lead of knowledge, the engagements of meanings. When we must act in ignorance, we pretend to know answers we do not have. Let us labor to increase our knowledge and our wisdom.

Listening to the Inner Voice

The World beyond These Walls
Inner Voice
An Inward Sign: Religion as a Feeling
What Being a Unitarian Universalist Means
The Conscience of a Unitarian Universalist
Being an Arrow in a Cyclical World
All is Sacred

The World beyond These Walls

We are urged, we feel moved, to use our empathy to project ourselves beyond our personal concerns and endeavor to help others. Perhaps even to change the world, at least a little.

There is an important sense in which we need to be aware that the community of love that we create within the church walls is dependent on people all over the world and some of those people are not doing nearly as well in their lives, in their education, in their health, as we are.

We pay special attention here to the Unitarian Universalists Service Committee and its projects and work, hopefully, to connect and focus ourselves with it.

One of the numerous ways in which we as Unitarian Universalists moved away from mainstream Orthodox Christianity of the Protestant faiths was to create the Unitarian Universalists Service Committee in 1939. The service committee is a different way of relating to other people in the world from that of evangelical Christians who think, or thought at that time, that the most important service they could offer was to send missionaries to convert people to Christianity. In their view and practice, whatever else was done for the condition of personal lives was frosting on the cake, the most important thing was their conversion to Christianity.

Our predecessors, as Unitarian Universalists, perceived that we needed to make a witness in the world, both here in the United States and elsewhere. But we chose to make a witness that was an enabling one, enabling people to do better in their lives than they presently were doing. We did not attempt, and we don't today, to manipulate people into becoming Unitarian Universalists or to give up any of their beliefs, religious or philosophical. Rather, we encourage people to stabilize their lives and to find ways of improving them with whatever help we have to offer.

The president of our denomination since the Unitarian Universalist merger in 1961, Bill Schulz, was concerned that focused religion needs symbols. In his column, *Finding Time*, in the *Unitarian Universalist World* magazine, Rev. Schulz points out that there are four symbols that are widely known by Unitarian Universalists, but no consensus on any. To direct our attention with more depth and significance, I am sharing some observations on the four symbols.

The Flaming Chalice

The source of the flaming chalice is thought to be Czechoslovakia—and not Czechoslovakia in recent times, rather Czechoslovakia in the 15th Century—when the first indications that a reform of the Christian Church was going to have to be undertaken; where courageous people first began to rebel against the conformity, the vacuous-ness, and the spiritual debasement of the existing Christian faith. At that time, Jan Huf emerged as a religious leader in Czechoslovakia. Huf felt that all believers should be able to drink from the chalice, not just priests— a radical view in that day. He was ultimately burned at the stake on orders from Rome for rebellious preaching. According to legend, he is said to have celebrated his own burning by saying that it would turn him into a light for the world and attract more attention to his views than if he had to promulgate them himself by traveling from village to village.

When our Service Committee was organized, the Flaming Chalice was adopted as a symbol of truth, the light of truth, and as a symbol of the purification that our religion intends to be about.

Interdependent Web

This symbol originated in St. John's Unitarian Universalist Church in the Ohio Valley District of the UUA. A proposal to incorporate it into our Unitarian Universalist Statement of Principles and Purpose [1984–85] came from Rev. Paul L'Herrou who was minister at St. John's in

Cincinnati. At the time, the concept of the Interdependent Web of All Existence was a significant endeavor to move away from the creativity of the transcendentalists, who proposed to discover the nature of reality by investigating the process of thought, rather than the objects of sense experience, and to search for reality through spiritual intuition. Our transcendental forebears altered the perceptions of people in their day, and in ours, about the individual's place in the world.

The price we have paid is an intense individualism which often makes it difficult for us to join together, to affirm each other as a group, and to acknowledge our dependency for life itself on lots of people who are not Unitarian Universalists. I think this affirmation of interdependency is long overdue.

The World

This represents the vision that was opened up to us when the astronauts moved out into space and the first photographs of earth from outer space were transmitted around the world. There is a deeply moving poem about the earth that was written and delivered by our Buckminster Fuller [American inventor and philosopher, 1895–1983], at that time:

> Dear God of Galaxies, we give thanks for being. We give thanks for being here. We give thanks for being here together, riders on the earth today, brothers and sisters in a bright loveliness in an eternal cold. With others, brothers, sisters, we all know now that we are truly, truly brothers and sisters.

The implication of our adventure into space certainly has reflected back to all of us the necessity of doing far more than taking care of our immediate premises, but of the added necessity of expanding our care to a stewardship for our city, for our state, for our nation, for our world.

Boston and Beacon Hill

Boston and Beacon Hill are *sacred spaces* to us even here in Indiana. There is some legitimacy to affirming our connectedness to Boston and to the immense cultural wealth that has come not only to us as Unitarian Universalists, but to people of all persuasions, religious and non-religious. This powerhouse of knowledge, of truth-seeking, of valuing human beings has been generated since Boston's early settlement. I think that anyone who visits or lives in Boston for a while gets some sense of a place that is in some way sacred to our history and to our national character.

There is another place in the world that is viewed as being sacred to us, and one about which we should all be troubled and concerned, Transylvania. (Transylvania is a place that we all know about because that is where Bela Lugosi dwelt—the home of the vampires!) Transylvania is a Hungarian-speaking, Hungarian-culture area, which for reasons that are not at all clear was assigned to be ruled by the government of Rumania after World War I and, I believe, was confirmed after World War II.

In Transylvania, we have Unitarian congregations more than four hundred years old; those congregations were established in 1568 in all villages of Transylvania by their king who had converted to Unitarianism, King John Sigismund I, the only Unitarian monarch in history. Many of these congregations exist to this day—some of the oldest Unitarian Congregations anywhere in the world.

The Rumanian government, in the name of modernization and tightening their cultural hold in Transylvania, plans to wipe out whole villages with bulldozers, including those beautiful old Unitarian churches, and build modern apartment dwellings instead. They claim this will open more land for agriculture and will provide more space for industry.

The outrage began to surface in the summer of 1988 as we gained the first information about this. I think this is a concern about a form of government and a concern about the rights of people all over the world to worship in ways that are most significant for them, and that we here must be concerned about what's going on in Transylvania.

The May/June 1990 issue of *Unitarian Universalist World* reports that a delegation visiting Rumania found that, following a revolution earlier that year, all religions can now be practiced freely in the *New Rumania*. Approximately 120 Transylvanian Unitarian Churches survived the repression that lasted from 1967–1989. Building repairs and new construction, along with membership growth, and a Sister Church Program with North America are in progress.

Spiral Galaxy Symbol

To the four symbols featured in Schulz's article, I would add Spiral Galaxy Symbol first proposed by Rev. Kenneth L. Patton, who established the Charles Street Meetinghouse in Boston as a center of Universalism in 1948 and, in a more contemporary sense, adopted the spiral galaxy photographs widely displayed in our churches. Our place in space is perhaps best exemplified by this. The spiral galaxy to my mind is not something to worship. It is something to inspire in us a kind of awe that is necessary but so often insufficient in contemporary life—an awe of our place, our tininess in space, and our dependence on systems far grander than what we can know or talk about.

There is an urgent need for us to gather our resources for continuing support of the deprived and the violently treated people in the world. How do we choose what to do? How we choose, I think, is to get as much information as we can, but not be overwhelmed by it.

The famous architect Mies van der Rohe said, "God is in the details."

We tend in our religion in the United States today to look for simplifications, to look for easy ways of recruiting people, for easy ways of focusing people's attention. All such simplifications are evil, or at least very deceptive, because this earth of ours, the people who live here, and everything we have to deal with are not simple. They are complex.

One of the things I find most important about Unitarian Universalist congregations across the United States is that the minister or the speaker is not expected to give simple bromide solutions to congregations or to provide easy answers. Simple solutions are, in and of themselves, suspect.

I think that what our church is here for us to shore up each of us to do those things that we can, and to help us continue to do the best things we can.

Related Reading

We have what blessedness there is on earth: living each day in fullness of life, thankful for what we have while we live. Leaving nothing unlived, we might have lived. Not cheated by our avenues of discontents, nor hoodwinked protected from bright reality by mirages of deluded faith. Having perceived many things in this life, living here in Eden, and knowing that it is indeed Eden here where we live, knowing this lifetime itself is eternity we are thus opened for the claim of the abundance of the world and our years in it. Having Earth and one another, we are blessed with all blessedness.

—Source unknown

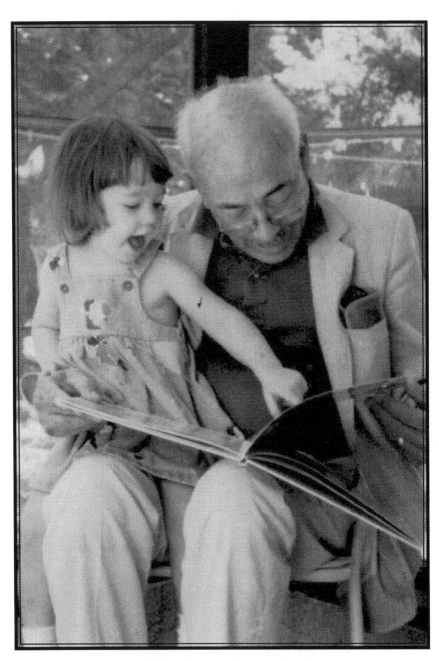

Dick and granddaughter Sara

Inner Voice

It is important that the modern world should realize how recent the discovery of character is. Civilization is built upon character and the foundations are still so new that we need feel no discouragement if the building has not yet exhibited the stability we may yet hope to see it achieve.

The marvel is that a creature rising out of animal savagery should have advanced to begin the great transformation at all. And it should give us all little concern that in carrying on its further development, people have at times faltered or even lost ground for a time.

Neither science, nor scientists, nor historians are evaluating the present situation in full recognition of the fact that the emergence of conscience as a social force is an event of yesterday. Moral development on our planet is an unfinished process and in this fact lies our greatest reason for hopefulness.

—*The Dawn of Conscience* by James Breasted, early 20th Century historian.

From our Unitarian Universalist perspective, Breasted's work remains one of the basic seminal understandings of how the human conscience is developed.

Today I think many of us would be less optimistic than Breasted in affirming that there has been steady progress over the last 4,000 years since the Egyptians first developed conscience; that each succeeding generation and government has improved upon that down to the present time.

We are more likely to agree with Breasted's premise that as human beings began to work together to establish cohesive, orderly, dependable government, the social fabric supported the development of *norms* in human beings and an understanding of *appropriate* behavior.

At the same time, there seems to be within us as human beings, God-given, divinely-granted or mysteriously developed through some kind of Darwinian evolution, a potentiality to look at social situations, to look at interpersonal situations, to look at governmental situations and decide that this mode of behavior is okay and this, not okay.

We, as Unitarian Universalists, tend to hold on to both views. We believe that conscience is both something that develops in fellowship or in community and that it is something God-given. So we have the innate conscience, refined, strengthened, enlarged through the socialization process.

Religion today, I think, is essential to us in a more renewed and invigorated way than it was in the last fifteen or twenty years.

Individuals are in a transition, our culture is in a transition, the world is in a major transition and the forms that religion of the future may manifest are mysteriously unknown to us. We need to be adapting. We need to be changing. We need, at the same time, to be affirming those things which we hold most deeply.

The conscience is at the center of all human activity. And the conscience needs to be informed and to direct rational, mature leadership: leadership that is rational, leadership that is intellectual, leadership that will participate in the ongoing re-definition of life and culture, and the inter-relationship between people in the world today.

Our challenge is to find new and better ways within the church, within our communities and within our national government to attract and put into office the people capable of such leadership.

One of the important books of the last thirty years is British journalist and historian Barbara Tuchman's *March of Folly* (1984). We find this in her introduction:

> A principle that emerges is that folly is a child of power. We all know from unending repetitions of Lord Acton's [British historian, 1834–1902] dictum that power corrupts. We are less aware that it breeds folly, that the power to command frequently

34

causes failure to think. That the responsibility of power often fades as its exercise augments. If rather than serving self-interest, the mind is open enough to perceive that a given policy is harming rather than serving self-interest and self-confidence enough to acknowledge it and wise enough to reverse it—that is the summit in the art of government.

I think, as a beginning, each of us needs especially to be aware of our ethical, moral voice within. Is that voice clear? Is it even functioning? Is it addressing the issues that lie before us? Is it giving us guidance? Are we sharing what it says with others openly? Are we seeking in whatever small way to make this a little better world?

All creatures in the wild are free, responsible for their sustenance and survival. Responsibility is a consequence of freedom. With no other power concerned for us, we do for ourselves or we are undone. We are responsible for what we make of the world and where we place ourselves in it. We are responsible for what we make of ourselves.

It is better to be powerless and impotent than to be powerful and damned. Where we love, we're most betrayed. Where we give, we receive the least. Only the person who loves us can deny us. Only the one who blesses us can curse us. Only the one who accepts us can reject us. Others neither accept nor reject, they ignore us.

Our responsibility is to give. Reception is another's task. We do what is ours to do. Our responsibilities are self-contained. To be free, to be self-established is the human goal. We have the universe; we have the village of the world. We are established in the great wheel in which all small wheels turn. The total vision of our race is the world, our continuity, our endurance.

Related Readings

We alone congratulate ourselves on our virtues and condemn ourselves for our sins; for we're responsible for the province of our being as we move freely upon our doings and our collaborations.

—Source unknown

Peace doesn't come through strength, strength comes through peace.

—William Sloane Coffin, Jr., American author

An Inward Sign: Religion as Feeling

Let us think about the question of religion and feeling. What is the relationship between the two concepts? What role should feelings play in religion? What should the relationship of our feelings be to our religion? To what do we refer when we use the word *feeling*?

When we employ the word *feeling*, most of us do so in a variety of ways, some of which are actually quite inappropriate. One legitimate definition of the word is that of *sensitivity*—that which we mean when we say, "You have hurt my feelings".

Feeling, in its precise meaning, always includes a physiological response, as the word itself suggests. In its primary usage, it refers to one of the five senses, that of touch; and in its more sophisticated usage, it denotes any partly-mental, partly-physical response marked by pleasure, pain, attraction, or repulsion.

It is significant to note that contemporary psychotherapists are increasingly emphasizing the recognition of the feelings—using the word in its precise sense—as the primary key to mental health and maturity. In their view, anxiety, anger, fear, and lust are the basic problem-causing emotions of human beings.

If we attempt to be equally specific in our use of the word *feeling* in connection with religion, two things are suggested: that men and women establish religions, or turn to ready-made religions, partly because of the discomfort they experience in connection with their feelings; and that responsible and effective religion, whatever its origin, helps humans to face their uncomfortable feelings, to come to terms with them, and thus to commit themselves constructively to participation in the life process in which we have been placed by God, our Creator.

On the one hand, students of the history of religions and of comparative religions and, on the other hand, anthropologists, have extensively debated whether religion originated in the feeling of joy or in the feeling of fear. True joy, of course, comes to us when we are able to accept our human condition: our proclivities to be anxious, to be fearful, to lust after any and all kinds of creature comforts—and to subordinate and direct these feelings toward constructive goals for the beloved human community.

This argument over the origin of religion is a chicken-and-egg kind of argument. The Biblical creation story tells us that we started out accepting ourselves and our human condition and then *fell* into the knowledge of anxiety, anger, fear and lust. Scientific evolutionists would have it the other way around—that what we are today is the fruition of a process in which we slowly emerged from a bestial condition—that the concept of the Garden of Eden is not a remembrance of things past, but a protective vision of the future.

However that may prove to be—if we are ever to fully know—it seems certain to me that religion, as Frederick Schleiermacher [German Protestant theologian 1768–1834] and Theodore Parker [American Unitarian clergyman and social reformer 1810–1860] perceived it a century ago, originated and originates in each of us in our sense of dependence upon each other and upon the sometimes incomprehensible whims of the physical universe in which we live.

The pacifying message of Norman Vincent Peale, 20th Century American clergyman and author of *The Power of Positive Thinking*, seems wrong to me in many respects. But it is particularly wrong in that it elevates humankind's most potentially destructive feeling, lust—lust for power, success and material affluence—into a goal. From earliest times, human beings have recognized and expressed the idea in all of the great religions of the world—Hinduism, Buddhism and Christianity—that acquisitiveness for its own sake is but a thinly disguised form of lust and can only lead to bitter frustration, and ultimately, if carried far enough, to destruction.

We Unitarian Universalists, with our Puritan tradition, have too often tended to deny the importance of our feelings, to suppress them completely under a thin veneer of rationalism, and thus to fall victim to a pride based on the false assumption that we have altogether conquered our feelings and have them fully under control.

Responsible religion is that religion which enables us to face our feelings openly, to recognize their potential for leading us into destructiveness and to channel such feelings into the concerns and causes which lead us to the recognition of God's love for each one of us. Creative religion neither panders to our feelings, nor deceives us into thinking that we can totally suppress them, as a rigidly rationalistic religion tends to do. Instead, it aids us to accept our dependence, our limitations as human beings, as the first step in the process of truly transforming ourselves and our world.

The American philosopher and psychologist William James, 1842–1910 wrote, "Be not afraid of life." But he did not hold out to us the false illusion that by conquering our fears with faith we therefore become entitled to success and wealth. Rather, the promise James held out for us is well expressed in this poem by George Santayana:

O world, thou choosest not the better part;
It is not wisdom to be only wise,
And on the inward vision close the eyes;
But it is wisdom to believe the heart.
Columbus found a world, and had no chart
Save one that faith deciphered in the skies;
To trust the soul's invincible surmise
Was all his science and his only art?
Our knowledge is a torch of smoky pine
That lights the pathway but one step ahead
Across a void of mystery and dread.
Bid, then, the tender light of faith to shine
By which alone the mortal heart is led
Unto the thinking of the thought divine.

**—George Santayana, *The Light of Faith,* Spanish-
American poet and philosopher, 1863–1952**

Related Readings

For everyone there are higher and lower levels of attainment; and whatever leads the individual to the higher level is worth believing in…A man's religion is the audacious bid he makes to bind himself to creation and to the Creator. It is his ultimate attempt to enlarge and to complete his own personality by finding the supreme context in which he rightly belongs.

—Gordon W. Allport, *The Individual and His Religion***, 1897–1967**

O God, remind us anew that the greatest of prophets and seers in all the ages are remembered best for their extensive capacities for feeling compassion for their fellow men. Guide us, we pray, to perceive more fully how we, in our limited ways, can enrich the lives of others through sympathetic, meaningful, concrete concern for each other, for the members of this community, for all members of the human community, whoever they may be.

—Source unknown

Help us in all of our thinking, our feeling, and our doing so to bear our parts in the work of the world that goodness, loving-kindness, and wisdom may be spread everywhere. Amen.

—Source unknown

What Being a Unitarian Universalist Means

Religious pluralism enriches and ennobles our faith; we're inspired to deepen our understanding and expand our vision, promising to one another our mutual trust and support. We believe in the many-faceted and incompleteness of truth; that truth is a process, something we endlessly seek.

We believe in the oneness, in the wholeness, in the interconnectedness of all of life, in all of its forms, in all of its expressions, physical, spiritual, emotional. We're connected to the earliest humanoids that existed on this planet; we're connected to people who hopefully will be dwelling here thousands of years from now. We're connected to all forms of animal life, to everything that exists giving significance to life. The kind of life that I live, the kind of life that you live, the kind of life that everyone lives is of central importance.

In our search for truths, in our seeking to harmonize truths and in our recognition of the interconnectedness of life, we endeavor to be very aware of the human condition. In our tradition, we seek to identify and enhance human potentialities and support human inclinations to create change for the better here on earth.

Our belief in the relative vitality and justice of the democratic process has a special kind of meaning. Part of our religious commitment is to the necessity of the democratic process. This explains our involvement in the political arena.

So far as Unitarian Universalists are concerned, being political is a blessed state. An important part of being a human being and being mature involves understanding the political process and participating in it. We affirm the democratic process as being essential to the significant practice of religion. We do this in part out of respect for the faith of individual people who come here. No two members of this congregation believe alike or think alike: not on spiritual matters, sometimes not on social matters, surely not on political matters. However, we believe that politics are unavoidable in human life, and that our participation is necessary.

We believe in the positive nature, the positive character of life. That life is good, that we are here for a good purpose, that it's desirable for us to make commitments to life, to affirm life and that it is necessary for us to live up to the commitments that we make and to keep them.

To review: Our belief is in the many-faceted and incompleteness of truth; in the holistic inner-connectedness of life and all its forms and expressions. We are keenly aware of the human condition and its potentiality, both for evil and for good. We believe in the relative vitality and justness created by the democratic process. And we affirm the positive character of life and the desirability of making commitments to life and living up to the commitments we make.

If one loves one's life, according to those precepts, one then needs to be open to other people and to the truths that they have; to affirm persons of different backgrounds, traditions, religions, ethnic connections; to learn about them. One must be sophisticated rather than naive about the potentiality for evil in the world—evil in the things you and I do, as well as the things that others may do to you or to me or to the United States. One also needs to be committed to the democratic process, to politics as part of religion. Finally, one must affirm life. Our religion cultivates those very characteristics that are desirable and necessary for people to survive and do well, and even to excel within the political process if that is what they choose to do.

My challenge to us all is not just to take pride in those people who are working and striving to make our culture and our nation and our world a somewhat better place in which to live, but to take responsibility for today.

I challenge each of you to give meaning to your faith and to mean what you do. That's what being a Unitarian Universalist really means.

The Conscience of a Unitarian Universalist

There is a great inequality in the degree of man's gift for science and technology on the one hand and for religion and sociability on the other, and this is, to my mind, one of man's chief discords, misfortunes and dangers. Human nature is out of balance. There has always been a *morality gap*, like the *credibility gap* of which some politicians have been accused. We could justly accuse the whole human race, since we became human, of a *morality gap* and I am convinced myself, that man's fundamental problem is his human egocentricity. He dreams of making the universe a desirable place for himself, with plenty of free time, relaxation, security, good health, and with no hunger or poverty

All the great historic philosophies and religions have been concerned, first and foremost, with the overcoming of egocentricity. At first sight, Buddhism and Christianity and Islam and Judaism may appear to be very different from each other, but when you look beneath the surface, you will find that all of them are addressing themselves primarily to the individual human psyche or soul; they are trying to persuade it to overcome its own self-centeredness and they are offering it the means for achieving this. They all find the same remedy. They all teach that egocentricity can be conquered by love.

We, as Unitarian Universalists, are sometimes criticized for not having a sufficiently deep conception of evil or of sin. We're a little like the psychoanalysts that Karl Menninger M.D., psychoanalyst 1893–1990, referred to, perhaps in the sense that we dislike the word *sin* because of the word's bad connotations!

Menninger writes: Conscience operates partly from the dark past, as it were, using strictures and sanctions from the childhood period, and remaining largely unconscious and inaccessible to new information. *Sin* is not a word much employed by psychoanalysts. It is implied in the adjective *aggressive* as applied to behavior, meaning purposely hurtful to others; Likewise, in self-destructive, purposely hurtful to oneself. It is taken for granted that either quality disqualifies an act, and marks it for elimination in the best interests of health. Psychoanalysts do not use the word *isn't* because of its strong reproachful quality, its vague or nonspecific quality, and its corollaries and implications of guilt, reparation and atonement. Why are aggression and self-destruction prima facie evils for the psychoanalyst to single out, or for that matter for anyone else; because both are opposed to the life principle, to the healing of the patient's disorganization and distress.

We're criticized that we skip lightly over the real evil in the world when we primarily deal with its social and psychological ramifications and their effects on our individual lives. While I acknowledge that this is true at least of some Unitarian Universalists, I don't think it's true of all clergy and/or all lay people as well.

I've always had some difficulty in reconciling with another judgment often made of us that we get too involved with trying to right the wrongs of the world. Now that's a real paradox! What are we faced with when we discuss the conscience of a Unitarian Universalist? How does the conscience of a Unitarian Universalist differ from other kinds of consciences?

First of all, there is the conscience that deals with rules, laws and codes. The basic rules, laws and codes which undergird our consciences as Unitarian Universalists as well as those of other peoples are the Ten Commandments, and the Seven Deadly Sins: envy, anger, pride, sloth, avarice, gluttony and lust. My conviction is that, whether or not we have chosen to move out of and beyond the Judaic-Christian tradition in our beliefs about religion, our own lives are largely governed by the principles and behavior codes of that tradition.

If, however, a Unitarian Universalist zealously applies the Ten Commandments or the Seven Deadly Sins, one particularly encounters many slippery value judgments in the area of marriage, remarriage and changed relationships in today's world. And if those principles were applied rigorously, they would not under any circumstances allow for separation, for divorce or for remarriage, which I think is inhuman.

I think, therefore, we are faced, so far as these Commandments and Seven Deadly Sins are concerned, to apply our reason which we extol so much as Unitarian Universalists, and ask how do these, how should these apply in this particular situation? How do they apply in my daily life, in my personal life? How do they apply in a social situation?

But I want to make a rejoinder here. I think sometimes there are some grounds for the charge that we are superficial about this. My principle is: don't break the rules as they're generally understood in society unless and until you have really thought through your reasons. Many of the problems that we face stem from the fact that we just don't think in terms of conscience. If it feels good, do it; if it doesn't feel good, don't do it—no matter what the consequences are for that *feel good*. That principle is not a principle that I think we can comfortably accept.

Joseph Fletcher, the American theologian, and his book *Situation Ethics*, is very useful to us as Unitarian Universalists. Yes, we accept traditional definitions of what is evil and what should not be, but we also educate ourselves to use our reason to evaluate individual, particular situations and to make a decision on the basis of that evaluation, often in dialogue with other people.

The Unitarian Universalist conscience, then, is to make thoughtful decisions, especially if one wants to go against the traditional rules, for certainly there are many rules that need to be changed and there is no question that we have far too many laws on the books, rather than too few. The amount of illegal behavior that we proscribe by law, therefore, ought to be specific and limited, and we ought to be able to comfortably live with those laws. If we can't, then we ought to set about to eliminate those laws. Even aggression and self-destruction need to be dealt with in terms of the current situations.

The challenge to us today, in the development of a conscience that really works, is to perceive that we need to air issues and to then involve ourselves, each of us in the process of defining our own position.

There are four ways in which we have conscience and in which conscience ought to work for us as Unitarian Universalists: be aware of the general rules of the codes, the guidelines of personal and social behavior; evaluate the code, evaluate the rule; evaluate the situation; and modify your stand so that it is clear to yourself and others. Take into account the importance of doing this in terms of the effect of your behavior, your decision, on a larger community, and work for change in this world. It is necessary, it is desirable, it is possible.

We must commit ourselves to a quality of judgment, using our reason, integrity and spirit. We alone congratulate ourselves on our virtues and condemn ourselves for our sins. We're responsible for the province of our being as we move freely upon our doings and collaborations.

Related Readings

Two things fill the mind with an ever-increasing wonder and awe, the more often and the more intensely the mind is occupied with them: the starry heavens above me, and the moral law within me.

—Immanuel Kant, philosopher, 1724–1804

All that is true, all that is noble, all that is just and pure, all that is lovable and gracious, whatever is excellent and admirable—fill all your thoughts with these things.

—*Philippians 4:8 NEB*, New Testament

The function of approving or disapproving what the instincts and the occasion impel one to do has long been called the conscience.

—Sigmund Freud, psychoanalyst, 1856-1939

Being an Arrow in a Cyclical World

Jesus' life is presented to us as one that had a beginning, middle and an end, like the path of an arrow in flight. Stephen Jay Gould, American scientist and educator, points out in his book *Time's Arrow; Time's Cycle,* [1987] that we characterize lives and epochs both as cycles and as arrows and we do this, most often, without some very clear sense of the possible disharmony which we are creating as we do so.

As Unitarian Universalists, it makes considerable difference which metaphor is dominant—the circle or the arrow. I refer to time's arrow and time's cycle as metaphors because Gould is developing an examination and an explanation as to why it has been so difficult for people since the 1800s to adapt adequately to an understanding that the universe is huge.

Prior to the 1700s, all thought of human beings was focused on the earth and on the immediate heaven, so the idea that time began about 5,000 years before Jesus was not difficult for human beings to grasp.

But when the effect of Galileo's observations, [Italian astronomer, 1564–1642], and of Newton's theories, [English mathematician, 1642–1727], really began to penetrate science and religion and the ordinary thinking of human beings, people generally said I do not want to deal with the possibility that the universe is billions of years old or that there are billions of planets or that there are billions of solar systems. Instead, people have preferred, in one way or another, to act as if this really isn't the case because if we accept the scientific view, our human history is a very narrow time in the course of the universe, as we now understand it.

To illustrate this concept a clergyman suggested that if you take a yardstick and hold it with arm outstretched and let that represent the entire extent of time that we now know to have elapsed, then the entire length of the yardstick is the time in which there were no human beings around.

And the time in which we, in our great history of ourselves, are significant is about the amount of flesh at the end of your middle fingernail.

This knowledge has had horrendous effects on human beings so far as psychology is concerned, so far as the meaning of religion is concerned, and so far as interpersonal relationships are concerned!

Gould cites Thomas Burnet, [an Anglican clergyman 1635–1715], who wrote about time, geological time and deep time, in the latter part of the 1600s. Gould also studies the work of James Hutton, [Scottish geologist 1726–1797], who produced work on deep time about a hundred years later in the 1780s in England, and the work of the English geologist Charles Lyell, undertaken in the 1820s and 30s. Gould ties it all together with a look at the Museum of Primitive American Art in Washington, D.C. In this museum, there is a fantastic creation by a man who was a janitor in Washington, D.C. This artistic janitor gathered various pieces of tin foil, cast-off fiber, wood chairs and tables, and put them all together to create a throne room for Jesus Christ to occupy when He returns for the Second Coming. This throne room epitomizes the desire of all of us in the 21st Century to hold on to some particular point of time, to give significance and interpretation to all that has gone on in the universe before now, and to predict what will subsequently happen to us.

Now back to deep time. The concept of deep time is an acknowledgment of the fact that what really counts—of the existence of the millennium of time—is only that which we can reconstruct theoretically from the scientific observation which engulfs all of us.

The most active deniers of deep time in our society today are the people whom we call the fundamentalists. They are the people who claim that everything that has ever actually happened only occurred in the last 5,000 years, from the time the earth was created as reported in Genesis, down to the present day. Consciously or unconsciously, they are making an effort to deny the existence of the universe as it is and to deny the existence of all time that has transpired before and up to now.

Deep time is also the tool of the people who term themselves scientific creationists, who purport to adopt the standards of science to study the geological formations and arrive at an affirmation of how old the earth really is, which is not very old actually.

The confusion Gould points to is that we, or any, splinter offspring of the Judaic-Christian tradition, also denied the existence of deep time—largely in the way we celebrate ourselves religiously. We, like the fundamentalists, affirm history. We too affirm that everything has a beginning, middle and an end. We like history. We evaluate lives on the basis of where they began; what were their prospects, what did the person with those prospects do with them.

On the other hand, Hinduism and Buddhism, because they have no sense of the historical, are cyclical religions based on a notion that time repeats itself; that everything repeats itself.

Gould's view is that we get ourselves engaged in the wrong kind of argument with the fundamentalist, or with the scientific creationist, because we're saying our history is better than your history. Our view of history is better than your view of history.

This suggests to me that it is possible we will continue to behave totally motivated by the arrow concept of time, and in ways that are not very productive for us. I think we have to absorb into our worship and into our personal lives some stronger understanding of the importance of a cyclical view of time and the universe—a view that affirms that there are some basic principles that are valid and have been valid through eons of time. And it's only because of those basic principles, which can be defined in scientific terms that we're able to carry on the scientific enterprise at all!

In other words, if everything is viewed as historic, we actually are saying that there are no principles with which to evaluate anything. Since everything happens once and only once, it's never going to be repeated. It happened. It's over. It's gone. Whatever happens to us is new and different. It's never happened to people before, so our attention ought to be fixed on making the most of the present.

Such thinking, I would also dare to suggest, is perhaps the creation of much of the dissatisfaction and dislocation that is occurring in Western Europe and in the United States; and the misunderstanding about who we are as a people and what we need, our misunderstanding of our relationship to the divine and to the universe.

Instead, we need to find some ways to meld both the arrow and the cyclical time metaphors in our thinking. We need to have some basis of evaluating history so that we are not simply repeating the mistakes of the past. We repeatedly make mistakes, done in by the cyclical character of time.

There are some basic principles that need to be held onto and affirmed, and some basic interconnections between Buddhism, Hinduism, Islamic religions and Christianity that can't simply be dismissed as "Those people are all superstitious nuts" and "It's our proper philosophical and theological view that will bring about the improvement of the world and of the species." We are historic human beings, unique and special, but we are also part of an ongoing history in which events do recur frequently enough for us to learn from the cycle.

Related Reading

Nature swings in nothingness until we contemplate it. And the meaning of nature endures while we give it meanings. Time and eternity are human offspring fastening the wheels of the stars in the images of our eyes. We count the stars that do not know how many they are. Space does not know *how far is space?* Time does not know *how long is time?* We carry the sun, our star, in the universe of our mind, bowing to the heavens, to time and space. They do not bow in return. Our courtesy is not lost for it lingers in the storehouses of our peace. So be it.

—Source unknown

All is Sacred

Dr. James Luther Adams, Professor Emeritus of Harvard Divinity School and one of our Unitarian Universalist greats, a major 20th Century figure in American religion, speaks very well to our Unitarian Universalist religion and what we try to be. These selections are from his sermon titled *Shalom, The Ministry of Wholeness*. It begins with a quotation from *Jeremiah 6:14*, ESV, "Everyone deals falsely. They have healed the wound of my people lightly saying *'Peace, peace,'* when there is no peace."

And then from *Luke 19:41* KIV, "And when he was come near, he beheld the city and wept over it, saying, if thou hadst known, even thou, at least in this thy day, the things *which belong* unto thy peace! But now they are hid from thine eyes."

Shalom, the word for peace is probably the Hebrew word most familiar to Gentiles. In Yiddish, the word is pronounced *show-lam* and in its most popular usage is the equivalent of hello or goodbye.

The question has been raised as to why the same word may be used for both hello and goodbye. The Israelis say it is because we have so many problems that half the time we don't know if we're coming or going.

In the form *Shalom Aleichem* the term means, *peace be with you*. In the scripture, however, the term is more than a salutation. It also means more than the absence of war. It's a profoundly religious term used to describe material and spiritual well-being, cognate with healthy, hale or whole.

Sometimes, God is spoken of as Shalom. In both the Old and New Testament, it is sometimes synonymous with the *Messianic Kingdom of God*.

For the ancient prophets, the word refers not only to the health or wholeness of the individual, but also to the health of a society—to the people as a corporate body under covenant. Sometimes the idea of corporate personality is implied, as though the society is a person capable of health or ill health.

The word shalom then possesses a striking breadth and depth, meaning the wholeness of authentic human life, God's intention for human beings and community. Shalom is holistic. Nothing is secular and beyond scrutiny. All is sacred.

Again, in the words from Jeremiah, "My people say, *Peace, Peace,* when there is no peace." The full force of the word shalom became electrically alive in the Nazi period in Germany where the common greeting imposed upon the nation was *Heil Hitler.*

A Christian professor of Old Testament at Marburg University paraphrased Jeremiah's words to read "My people say *Heil, Heil* and they know not what they mean." This paraphrase of the Jewish prophet Jeremiah was calculated to bring scorn upon the anti-Semitism of the Nazis, and it did so. All over Germany, especially in Christian anti-Nazi groups, the professor's translation was quoted.

Although the Old Testament was no longer read in pro-Nazi churches and the photograph of Hitler, the Jew Hater, was placed on the altar in some churches, the memory of the Jew Jeremiah was still alive. In the Nazi context, Jeremiah might justly excoriate those who deal falsely by attempting to *heal the wound of my people lightly* and daubing a gloss over the wound to peace, to wholeness. In the view of Jeremiah, the society thereby remains a suffering patient.

So, what then is wholeness? It is concern for the whole as well as for the parts: the recognition that no individual, no congregation may consider itself an isolated entity. The wholeness can exist only where justice and mercy are freely sought after. The integrity of the individual is bound up with the integrity of society. Shalom is holistic.

It is noteworthy that in some churches today, in Central and South America, one of the remarkable movements is that of liberation theology, liberation from the imprisonment of classism, racism, and sexism.

It is the position of Liberation Theology and the Catholics and Protestants who adhere to it, that we cannot be whole persons in unjust institutions. In such institutions, human potential is fragmented and distorted; human potential is stifled. And here, again, we must distinguish between the serious commitment to social change and the entertainment of noble virtues and attitudes. Kindly and seemingly generous attitudes do not suffice for wholeness. Institutional change, not beautiful attitudes, is what is required.

~

Related Readings

The world is a mirror of infinite beauty, yet no one sees it. It is a temple of majesty, yet no one regards it. It is a region of light and peace, unless we disquiet it.

You never enjoy the world aright, til the sea itself floweth in your veins; you are clothed with the heavens and crowned with the stars, and perceive yourself to be the sole heir of the whole world.

—Thomas Traherne, English clergyman, writer and poet, 1637–1674

> The children of humanity are one
> And I am one with them;
> I seek to love, not hate;
> I seek to serve and not exact due service;
> I seek to heal, not hurt.
> Let pain bring due reward of light and love;
> Let the soul control the outer form,
> And life and all events;
> And bring to life the love that underlies
> The happenings of the times.
> Let vision come and insight;
> Let the future stand revealed;
> Let inner union demonstrate
> And outer cleavages begone.
> Let love prevail;
> Let all people love

—A Tibetan Mantra

Choosing to Face the Truth

The Human Journey from the Heart
How and What to Forgive
Idealism without Innocence
Press on to the Emerald City
What is Prophethood?
Vive La Difference
The Devil: Myth or Monster

The Human Journey from the Heart

From the Bible, *Revelations 21:1–4: NEB:*

> I saw a new heaven and a new earth, for the first heaven and the
> first earth had vanished, and there was no longer any sea. I saw
> the holy city, New Jerusalem, coming down out of heaven from
> God, made ready like a bride adorned for her husband. I heard a
> loud voice proclaiming from the throne: "Now at last God has his
> dwelling among men! He will dwell among them and they shall
> be his people, and God himself will be with them. He will wipe
> every tear from their eyes; there shall be an end to death and to
> mourning and crying and pain; for the old order has passed away!"

From *Revelations 21:22-25 NEB:*

> I saw no temple in the city... and the city had no need of sun or
> moon to shine upon it...By its light shall the nations walk, and the
> kings of the earth shall bring into it all their splendour. The gates
> of the city shall never be shut by day—and there will be no night.

This reading describes the great vision of John of Patmos which has been
preserved for us in the New Testament Book of Revelations, the vision of
the culmination of time, the escheating of history, the descent of the great
holy city Jerusalem from heaven. It is interesting that, when this reading is
stripped of its supernatural language, it holds out before us a vision of the
future, a dream for us that encompasses many of our deepest hopes: a city
in which there shall be no tears, no mourning, no pain; a city suffused by
glorious light in which all the nations of the earth walk together in trust,
in and out, through gates which are open to everyone of every background.

In practice, however, this vision has most generally been held out to us as a promise for life after death. It is actually accompanied by threats of eternal punishment in a luridly conceived hell for those who refuse to give their highest loyalty, which refuse to make their ultimate commitment to a particular form of religion, to a particular creed or to a particular church. This has inevitably led to two evil results: (1) idolatry of some particular church as the only possible way to salvation; and (2) indifference toward or even hostility to life in this world.

The effect of this on us all has been that the great churches of Christendom and all the great religions of the world have placed a low valuation on human life, on the possibility and desirability of improving and reforming our worldly institutions.

The most liberal Christian denominations, the Hindu sects, and the Buddhist sects, have ultimately found themselves to be in conflict on this matter. Loyalty to their creed, to their conceptions of life after death, coupled with fear of death and of eternal punishment in hell, has crippled and hobbled their every effort to make of this world the best possible place in which we can live out our lives.

What, then, does this suggest to us about the need for and function of this church, of all of our kind of churches? It means that we join together in affirmation of our ultimate commitment of loyalty to the universal ideal of the human community. We affirm our faith in the possibility of humanity to bring this community into existence.

We meet together as a worshiping congregation for three purposes: to perceive what purposes are open to us as human beings; to sustain our hopes for the accomplishment of those purposes; and, to symbolize, to represent, to make concrete before the community this vision which we perceive.

The American theologian, H. Richard Niebuhr, 1894–1962, defined three kinds of faith: Henotheism—belief in or worship of one god without denying the existence of others; Polytheism—belief in or worship of more than one god, or many gods; and Monotheism—doctrine or belief that there is only one god.

It seems to me that we, as Unitarians, are radical monotheists in the sense that we affirm our loyalty to a center of values for humans above and beyond all existing values. But we know that our high ideals are elusive. The way to a universal community is fraught with difficulty. Let us remember, when we feel discouraged, these lines from *Isaiah 40:31;...* "those who look to the Lord will win new strength, they will grow wings like eagles; they will run and not be weary, they will march on and never grow faint."

Therefore, with loyalty and trust in our vision for humanity, we shall occasionally mount up, full of inspiration about our cause, with wings of eagles; perhaps more often we shall run for our cause without becoming weary; but, most of our lives, we shall be called upon to walk, patiently and tirelessly, but never fainting.

We all hold in our heart a dream for the world, for ourselves, for our children and for our friends. But each of us realizes that every human being is somehow interdependent with every other human being; that this dream will never be fully realizable for any of us until it is realized by everyone living everywhere in the world.

On our journey through life in this world, each of us is attempting to bring this dream for the community of humanity to a fuller realization. It is this dream, this vision which must command our highest loyalty, which is our center of value. We should try to make our church, in every possible way, an expression of our vision of humanity's ultimate goal as we journey according to our hearts.

~

Related Reading

A tree that it takes both arms to encircle grew from a tiny rootlet. A many storied pagoda is built by placing one brick upon another brick. A journey of three thousand miles is begun by a single step.

**—Lao–Tzu, Chinese philosopher, reputed
founder of Taoism, 604 B.C.**

How and What to Forgive

In the Bible [*Romans 12:1–2, 12:9–13 NEB*] there are passages about knowing your place in life, being humble, being forgiving and being a doormat kind of human being:

> Therefore, my brothers, I implore you by God's mercy to offer your very selves to him: a living sacrifice, dedicated and fit for his acceptance, the worship offered by mind and heart. Adapt yourselves no longer to the pattern of this present world, but let your minds be remade and your whole nature thus transformed. Then you will be able to discern the will of God, and to know what is good, acceptable, and perfect.

> Love in all sincerity, loathing evil and clinging to the good. Let love for our brotherhood breed warmth of mutual affection. Give pride of place to one another in esteem. With unflagging energy, in ardour of spirit, serve the Lord. Let hope keep you joyful; in trouble stand firm; persist in prayer. Contribute to the needs of God's people, and practice hospitality.

In my early adulthood, as I came to learn more about Christianity, I learned that self-abasement (from the very beginning of Christianity) was cultivated as an ideal for some. And we should not lose sight of the fact that the Reformation instituted by Martin Luther [German leader of the Protestant Reformation, 1483–1546] and John Calvin [French Protestant theologian of the Reformation, 1509–1564] was not, to begin with, a search for or a stand for, religious liberty, although it has come to signify that to us today. Rather, the Reformation was a protest against the commercialization that had occurred over humility and forgiveness. Martin Luther's great issue was a fight against the *indulgences*; the various ways people could give money to avoid having to be so humble and forgiving. Both Luther and Calvin objected to this, strenuously.

One of the positive fruits of the Bible scholarship in the 19th and 20th centuries has been to perceive that this passage from Romans 12:19: "Do not seek revenge, but leave a place for divine retribution." If read with a detached viewpoint, is quite another matter than fundamentalist Christians have been led to believe.

The term *interim ethics* was introduced by Albert Schweitzer, [Alsatian theologian, musician and medical missionary, 1875–1965], and it has stood the test of time pretty well. Now, what did that mean? It meant that people believed that the end of the world was very near and that it was their task to be self-effacing, to be humble, to be loving and forgiving; but remember, they believed they were going to get their reward and pretty soon, God was going to take care of their enemies. (It wasn't that they didn't have enemies; they simply were not going to take any action against them because they are promised at the end of this passage in Romans, that God will take care of them.)

This worked for a while in early Christianity, but eventually people lost faith in this particular tactic. We have witnessed, through 2000 years of Christianity, the reappearance from time to time of small sects that cultivate this kind of ethic in a totalistic way, because they are again convinced that the end of the world is about to come, for one reason or another.

The other fruit of the 19th and 20th Century's Biblical criticism was to perceive that both Jesus and Paul were very aggressive men (something that had been lost sight of in 1300 years). They may not have been aggressive in the sense of being fist fighters or soldiers, but they were extremely aggressive and judgmental about people. Our position on this issue, of course, has been that the teachings of Jesus were the important elements in the matter. In the 20th Century: however, we—together with many people in our society—have come more and more, when thinking about aggression, into trying to understand it in psychological terms.

Dr. Fredric Wertham [Chief Assistant Psychiatrist at Johns Hopkins Hospital in Baltimore and Senior Psychiatrist at Bellevue in New York City] says, "The theory that is often expressed that we are little more than animals and consequently, aggression is simply part of human nature, is one that I have little patience for."

Wertham opposes Oswald Spengler, who told the German people two years before Hitler came to power that "the tactics of man's life is that of a splendid grey, cunning, cool beast of prey. He lives attacking, killing, and destroying: he has wanted to be master as long as he has existed."

Well, as 20th Century people, we are faced in our search for values with a radical reappraisal of traditional humanistic values, with a radical reappraisal of psychoanalytic values and with a radical appraisal of aggression and violence. I think that the thesis that man is aggressive is one we will have to begin with and act upon. This does not mean that we will make a virtue out of aggression; but on the other hand, we must recognize that almost every accomplishment of any significance has been made because someone had the aggressiveness and the willingness to push ahead. We can't, however, continue to hold with the old humanistic thesis, which Dr. Wertham explicates, that a human being is perfectible if you continue to hold up values before him. (Just be good enough, kind enough, thoughtful enough and everything will turn out all right!)

We have to come to terms much more realistically it seems to me, with the aggressive person that is in each of us, directly or indirectly expressed. As the Austrian zoologist Konrad Lorenz [1903–1989] reminds us, "We are the missing link, not the end of evolution."

This, then, is not the positivistic theory of Spengler or the Nazis at all, but a recognition with humility that we are little more than animals and not the end of evolution.

Now, what and how, then, do we forgive? I'll give you one example of a creative and constructive way that sets a tone that I would like to emulate. (Granted, it's not a way that is specifically open to all of us.)

In 1930, Gandhi led the Salt March to protest the salt tax in India, and after the rioting of troops and so forth, Gandhi was called in to speak with the Viceroy, Lord Erwin from London. The Viceroy invited Gandhi to have a cup of tea with him. Now, Gandhi had a wonderful sense of humor and liked to tease people. So Gandhi accepted the cup of tea, and then from under his little white sheet that he always wore, he reached in and pulled out a tiny bag of illegal salt which he had brought with him. He sprinkled the salt into the tea as a reminder, he said, of the famous Boston

Tea Party. I think that is an excellent example of how to be aggressive and at the same time forgiving.

In the search for values, the 20th Century person needs to practice humility, repentance and forgiveness. I think these are essential for getting along well with each other. It is our additional responsibility to redefine these principles more radically than they have been for us in the past, or that we have succeeded in doing so far.

Idealism without Innocence

Throughout my life, I've sought to remain idealistic despite my early and pretty funny, pretensions to being sophisticated and otherwise. In some small ways, I have succeeded, I think... Nevertheless, it is a risk of this profession, I have often been told that involvement in idealist causes is an impossible, worthless endeavor, a waste of time. But, perhaps I can convert a few people to my way of looking at the world and so help to effect a few additional changes.

There is a very clear distinction between one's ideals and what one can accomplish in reality; between one's ideal of social life, what it ought to be, and what one can accomplish in practicality. And it's that distinction, that tension that constantly exists between our ideals and how we behave to our family, how we behave in our job, what we're connected with, that creates much of the tension in human society. It always has and it still does.

Somehow, I have had working for me a view, and that view seems to first have been uttered by the Reverend Sydney Smith in London in the 19th Century in his book, *The Memoirs of The Lady Howland*. What Smith said was, "Take short views, hope for the best, and trust in God."

The German philosopher Immanuel Kant [1724–1804] said, "Happiness is not an ideal of reason." His point, as I understand it, is that just because you think things through, because you work out the best possible way that life ought to be, no matter how carefully and intelligently you do it, it is not going to bring you any happiness—or very little. It may bring you some other kinds of satisfaction. "Happiness," Kant said, "comes from our imaginations."

I agree. Happiness comes from our ability to envision a world better than the one in which we live. Happiness comes from our experiencing among ourselves, with our families, with our neighbors, with our friends, a love that is mutually reinforcing in the life we lead. Such a love brings no guarantees that we're going to succeed in this endeavor or reach that goal, but it does give us the power to continue to try to sort out what's the best or the better and devote ourselves energetically to trying to achieve it.

Madeleine L'Engle demonstrates in her books that one needs, one must devise, must allow and set ways to play, to be playful, and to do mindless activities occasionally. I think also what sustains us are the various kinds of cultural activities in which we participate or which we share with each other—all of these provide, some healing sort of serenity when the challenges of life seem to be all but impossible.

You may have seen a very moving film about the changes in Czechoslovakia under the Soviets, and then the Soviets tightening up the power and driving more liberal people away from Prague. The title of the book and film (1984) is *The Unbearable Lightness of Being.* One of the lines by author Milan Kundera: "We can never know what to want, because living only one life we can neither compare it with our previous lives nor perfect it in our lives to come."

Having only one life to live is something that it has taken me all my life to understand. That this life and whatever I've done with it is the only life I've had, or am likely to have in the future. But that thought—that view—now sustains me and gives me energy when I feel as if I'm doing some rather hopeless things like shoveling sand against the tide. I think it's an important concept, essential for us all to believe, to share with each other, to pass on to our children.

Madeleine L'Engle, in talking about doing responsible things, doing creative things, doing moral things, says: "We all feed the lake."

All of us, together, feeding the lake is important. It's part of enlarging the human potential, a corporate act of humanity.

Related Readings

The arts and strategies of slaughter contribute nothing to wisdom. Carnage is never the way to peace. The lives lost in wars pass without retrieval from the deadly costs. After all our debacles, we must at last return to love, to the womb, to the songs and the peace of home.

—Source unknown

How does one separate the art from the artist? I don't think one does. And this poses a problem. How do we reconcile atheism, drunkenness, sexual immorality, with strong beautiful poetry, angelic music, transfigured painting?...The Russian novelist Dostoyevsky's [1821–1881] magnificent theology is not always compatible with his agonized life. Mozart [Austrian composer, 1756–1791] wrote one of his merriest and most joyful pieces while he was frantic over his dying mother. Mendelssohn [German composer, 1809–1847], who helped Bach [German composer, 1685–1750] give his Christianity to the world, was a Jew....Carl Jung [Swiss psychologist and psychiatrist, 1875–1961] says that we are far more than a part of ourselves than we can know about and that one of the most crippling errors of 20th Century culture has been our tendency to limit ourselves to our intellect.

—Madeleine L'Engle, *Walking on Water—*
Reflections on Faith and Art

The human mission is to balance good over evil...Our righteousness is to work for life in creativity, for we are saved by what we do and what we are....The way to joy is to love those we love, to succor those we cherish, to serve those who are ours to serve, to add an ounce of mercy to the scale of history, to give our medicines for the health of the world. In so doing, we restore our own sense of goodness and we believe in humanity, because we believe in ourselves. We give an edge to compassion over cruelty, to industry over sloth, to strength over weakness, to success over failure, to love over hate. We dispel some of the shame of history, some of our horror; to be ourselves prevailing over our shame—to be more fully human.

—Kenneth L. Patton, Unitarian Universalist
minister and author, 1911–1994

Press on to the Emerald City

In 1929, Dr. Edward Wagenknecht, one of the early scholarly officiators of L. Frank Baum and *The Wizard of Oz*, wrote of the Land of Oz as an American Utopia: "By this I do not mean that the Oz books are full of social criticism. Since they were written for children, this is obviously not the case: Yet the utopia element in them is strong. It would not be a bad thing if American lawmakers and executives were to imbibe a few of the ideals which actuate the lovely girl ruler of the Emerald City, Ozma of Oz." From Baum's book, *The Emerald City of* Oz, a brief description of Oz as Utopia occurs:

> Emerald City is built of all beautiful marble in which are set a profusion of emeralds. It has 9,654 buildings in which live 57,318 people. All the surrounding country, extending to the borders of the desert which enclosed it on every side, was full of pretty and comfortable farm houses in which resided those inhabitants of Oz who preferred country to city life. All together there were more than a half million people in the Land of Oz.
>
> Every inhabitant of that favored country was happy and prosperous. No disease of any sort was ever known, so no one ever died unless he met with an accident that prevented him from living. This happened very seldom, indeed. There were no poor people, because there was no such thing as money and all property of every sort belonged to the ruler. The people were her children and she cared for them. Each person was given freely by his neighbors whatever he required for his use, which is as much as anybody could reasonably desire. Some tilled the lands and raised great crops of grain which was divided equally among the entire population, so that all had enough.

Baum's *Oz* adapts itself quite readily to looking at some of the traditional utopias that human beings have been writing about and constructing since earliest time.

Utopia, as a word, is a name of a country in one of the great literary, intellectual flowerings of the English Renaissance period when humanism was at its height in the 16th Century. Sir Thomas More [English humanist, 1473–1535] wrote *Utopia*, a book which was a statement of his dreams and aspirations and hopes for human beings living in the world of the 16th Century, especially living in the world of England.

And the word *utopia*, the title of his book, has come to be common currency in our language and to be applied to all such thinking and writing. But he was by no means the first to engage in such concepts.

An obvious earlier example is Plato's *Republic* written in the 5th Century B.C. Plato, the great Greek philosopher, and some would say one of the greatest minds of all time, detailed how the ideal state should be organized, how it should be operated, and how people would function there. How Plato's ideal state would bring about more harmonious human relationships and an ideal world, is quite similar in more than a few respects, to the world pictured in Baum's Emerald City.

It's significant for us to recognize also the Book of Isaiah, which is a book of three identifiable different sections, presumably written by different people at slightly different times or places. It all comes from the 8th or 7th Century B.C. at a time after the triumphant reigns of King David and King Solomon when the ancient nation of Israel came apart. Isaiah is a book which urges the people of Israel to gather together to form a new covenant with each other and to reform to create a new world. This book holds up a tremendous vision of a new world, a new Jerusalem, which indeed should be heaven on earth, a world in which there would be plenty for all and peace for everyone. And there would be no battling, no wars, and all would be reconciled under God in recognition of God as the one ruler of the universe.

This is reflected again in the New Testament vision, in certain passages from Jesus, and from the New Testament books of the Gospels, and the story of the early Christians in Acts, where people indeed attempted to establish a kind of utopian community.

This has been true throughout religious history in the United States. There have been many such utopian communities, not just dreamed about but actually established, and people have endeavored to make them work.

New Harmony, Indiana, was the site of two different experiments of this sort. The first one worked much better than the second one, because it had a very patriarchal, dictatorial ruler and he saw to it that everybody played fair and that everybody did a day's work. Certainly, it was not the kind of open, anarchistic society in which it was presumed that everyone who was in this community was basically a good person and that their needs and wants and expectations were diverse enough and complementary enough to get everything done that needed to be done.

We do, however, continue to hold to a vision that somehow it is conceivable that at some distant time we will become transformed as human beings into creatures who are able to live together in this way.

And that indeed is the dream that's held up at the end of the New Testament in Revelations Chapter 21. It's a reiteration of the dream of Isaiah that there shall be a New Jerusalem and there shall be plenty for everyone. There shall be peace for everyone. The world will be ruled by God in love and reconciliation and we all will be one with each other.

The Emerald City, then, is very much in this tradition. The Oz books are about an invented world, a created world that's held up as an ideal.

What are the characteristics of the ideal city or country that are significant to us, to our own hopes and dreams and aspirations? Human beings and human cultures do not survive without hopes and dreams and affirmations, no matter how unrealistic they may be. No matter how many times they have failed, we all need hopes and dreams and aspirations. Even though we can point to all the utopias that have failed, there is something deep within each of us that says someday, some way, somehow, we are going to succeed in making this a better world than it presently is.

And what are some of those characteristics? One is that all utopias are based on some conception of material prosperity and physical comfort. Everybody has enough to eat, a comfortable place to live and sleep, and their material wants are looked after. How this is accomplished may be very communal; it may be accomplished also through barter, through trade, through free trade. But the desired end is for everybody to have enough and for there to be no poverty.

Another characteristic of a utopian society is a balance between rural and urban dwellers, who do not act in conflict with each other. A balanced kind of life, then, would be one where one can choose to be an urban dweller or to live in the country, where both are held in equal esteem, offering benefits for different people with different tastes. This is an ideal long held in America, but it is under a great deal of question today and there is a lot of tension to preserve it.

Still another characteristic of most visions of utopia is that they be physically beautiful places. Somehow their designers imply, it is part of our relationship with the Divine, with God, with the ultimate concerns that we should create, sustain and maintain things of beauty. Aesthetic attractiveness is an essential element in a utopia.

All utopias, of course, are committed to peace. Peace is a human want, a human ideal, a human desire that cannot be suppressed.

Another characteristic of a visionary society is one in which no labor is harsh or restrictive. There are no odious bosses. No taskmasters. All the work of the world is somehow enjoyable to somebody.

And finally, again the Biblical vision of utopia: there's no death, or very limited death. Living forever has been a human dream since the beginning of writing. We find it everywhere. This dream has been explored psychologically, sociologically; it's there in many, many forms, in our human literature and in all our utopias.

Within each one of us, there is a very personalized dream, a personal utopian state. There is this wonderful quote from Wagenknecht. He says: "The principle underlying what happens to the scarecrow and the tin man and the cowardly lion is the following: Man doesn't live by bread alone; but principally by catch words."

What does this mean? That we have societal cliches? I'd like to do that but I don't have the brains? Or I'm not bighearted? Or I'm a coward?

The point that I want to make here is that all three of these storybook characters are very different from the way they perceive themselves. It's the cliches that are keeping them from recognizing that they already have the very thing they're looking for.

There's a lesson here: a lot of life is overcoming the catch words that we tend to get ourselves hooked on, and put ourselves down with, which prevent us from seeing ourselves at full value.

There are also institutional utopias. And our dreams, our desires for ourselves as a congregation are those things that we hold together as an institution. All of these concerns of Utopia we need to be addressing in an institutional way. We need to preserve with all of our energy the imagination and sense of wonder which is a peculiar hallmark of L. Frank Baum's work. We must hold onto this great wonder at the world as it is and the wonder and imagination of how it might be—no matter how imaginary or impractical or unrealistic the vision may seem. Utopia is a vision that most human beings have held onto down deep in their hearts for thousands of years. It is when we lose sight of that vision that the world often is coming apart at the seams. So it's especially important to preserve our visions and our hopes, to sustain each other in a variety of ways to keep this church a place of visions and hopes and dreams, as practicalities.

These following words are on a card we give to visitors. They are realistic, but yet they are dreams and inspiration:

> Unitarian Universalism is a fierce belief in the way of freedom and reverence for the sacred dignity of each individual. With Jefferson we have sworn eternal hostility against every tyranny over the mind.

> Unitarian Universalism is cooperation with the universe that created us; it is a celebration of life; it is being in love with goodness and justice; it is a sense of humor about absolutes.

> Unitarian Universalism is faith in people, hope for tomorrow's child, confident in the continuity that spans all time. It looks not to a perfect heaven, but toward a good earth. It is respectful of the past, but not limited to it. It is trust in growing and conspiracy with change. It is spiritual responsibility for a moral tomorrow.

Related Readings

Meanings are a passport to wherever, opening travel to far prairies of space, importing the nebula into the small observatory of the brain, inhabiting the ark of understanding with every creature, assembling within us the universe for a seed.

Living is discovery: each moment fresh and undisclosed. Our discoveries never ended break forth every day. The years teach the feet of the climbers to climb. The days teach the eyes of the seers to see. Hills and valleys stretch out to be known—to the eye, an enticement; to the feet, a delight. The mind can no more exhaust the forage of the world than the holiday outing of a child can explore the shores of seven oceans. We have little time to relive the past with new days waiting to be lived.

—Kenneth L. Patton, *Hymns of Humanity,*
Unitarian Universalist minister, 1911–1994

Humanism is a progressive life stance that, without supernaturalism, affirms our ability and responsibility to lead thoughtful, ethical lives capable of adding to the greater good of humanity.

—American Humanist Association, 2014

What is Prophethood?

What is prophethood? What are the concepts of the priesthood of all believers, and the prophethood? The Reformation, 16th century religious movement which resulted in the establishment of Protestant Churches, was aimed among other things at reducing the power and the influence of the clergy of the Church of Rome as it was then experienced. Through personal reading of the Bible, which had become possible because of the invention of the printing press, Christians, (led by Martin Luther, John Calvin, and many others) perceived that priesthood alone should not have total control of the church. Luther and Calvin reasoned that all believers had something of the divine in them or accessible to them. They maintained that lay persons could lead worship and perform other functions—with the provision that the congregation itself had adequate awareness of its beliefs and acted as a decision-making body.

Unitarian Universalists, from the 1930s on, follow the practice of gathering a group of lay people who either are or want to become, active believing Unitarian Universalists. When there are about twenty such people, they can join together and create an organization, which we refer to as a *fellowship*. They do not have to call a minister. In the states of Indiana and Ohio, it is possible to perform those duties required of the church with lay people for the most part. So, this practice of the priesthood of believers has real applicability to us.

And these words from Dr. James Luther Adams, esteemed Professor Emeritus of Christian Ethics, Harvard Divinity School, from his essay *The Prophethood of All Believers:*

> A church that does not concern itself with the struggle in history
> for human decency and justice, a church that does not show

concern for the shape of things to come, a church that does not attempt to interpret the signs of the times, is not a prophetic church.

We have long held to the idea of the priesthood of all believers, the idea that all believers have direct access to the ultimate resources of the religious life and that every believer has the responsibility of achieving an explicit faith for free persons. As an element of this radical laicism we need also to affirm belief in the prophethood of all believers.

The prophetic liberal church is not a church in which the prophetic function is assigned merely to the few. Hope is a virtue, but only when it is accompanied by prediction and by the daring venture of new decisions....Humanity can surpass itself only by surpassing itself.

What does Dr. Adams mean when he says we should also describe our function as a prophethood of all believers? I believe he is affirming, as a Unitarian Universalist, the Christian message as exemplified by some of the teachings of Jesus that as religious people we should have the experience of freedom: freedom from the necessity of being sinful or evil, freedom from the necessity of being confused and freedom from putting ourselves into a hierarchy of people in which we rank very low and others are highly exalted. The issue for believers, in Dr. Adams' view of the Christian message, is that we must affirm our belief in human freedom as a central reason for the existence of our church.

We also affirm that the purpose and reason for religion is to establish freedom through cleaving together. *Cleaving together* is a term that is much used in Protestant religion. It's an interesting verb because it refers both to splitting things asunder, as in using a meat cleaver, and to *hanging together*. So, we Unitarian Universalists separate ourselves from each other, affirming our individuality, which is a key tenet in Unitarianism and in Universalism. At the same time, we are aware that we must hold onto each other, hang together as a group—because separately we cannot achieve this human ideal of freedom through the practice of religion.

Freedom cannot be acquired for ourselves on an individual basis. It only comes through the affirmation of our colleagues, our friends, our culture, that we indeed are free people. So, what are the functions of the prophet to bring about such freedom? The first function that I want to emphasize is discernment.

Dr. Adams has said that we are incurably religious. Thus, the central religious problem is not atheism, but it is idolatry—that is, not the absence of faith but believing in and worshiping the wrong things!—so, the need for discernment.

The faith that underlies the responsibility to discern the serious from the frivolous is a faith in the power of love to increase justice for all. If we want to use or to be understood in terms of traditional religious language, it is in this way that we as Unitarian Universalists seek and find salvation.

Salvation doesn't come through worship or through prayer all by itself. Salvation doesn't come through private virtues that camouflage public interest—rather it comes through time and history, through our recognition that history is fraught with judgment and fulfillment.

Authentic prophetism always demands some personal cost. Prophetism lays on us a religion that expects us to pay, to attribute and focus our lives in ways that may cost us something and often does. Ours, then, is a religion of action and of will, but it is also of meditation and of compassion. In the words of Dr. Adams, "I call that church free which does not cringe in despair, but casting off fear, is lured by the divine persuasion to respond in hope to the light that has shown and that still shines in the darkness." —*The Prophethood of All Believers,* Postscript: *The Church That Is Free.*

We respond in hope to the light that has shone and continues to shine in the darkness in the world—that is a free church to which we are committed.

~

Related Readings

Sometimes our light goes nearly out, but it is blown back into flame sometimes a brighter flame than ever before—by an experience or by an encounter with another human being. Let each of us be especially aware of the potentialities of life—for the rekindling of our inner lights. The more profound a religion is, the more it realizes this fact—that what it knows through belief is little compared to what it does not know.

—Albert Schweitzer, Alsatian theologian, musician and medical missionary, 1875–1965

We are early children of the race in the dawn of the human morning. For the human story awaits the filling of blank pages. We come, not to dedicate a finished house, but builders seeking stone and wood—architects—using our minds for a new plan.

—Source unknown

A young man ran and told Moses that Eldad and Medad were [prophesying] in the camp, whereupon Joshua son of Nun, who had served with Moses since he was a boy, broke in, "My Lord Moses, stop them!" But Moses said to him, "Are you jealous on my account? I wish that all of the Lord's people were prophets and that the Lord would confer his spirit on them all!" And Moses rejoined the camp with the elders of Israel.

—*Numbers 11:27–31 NEB*

Vive La Difference

Occasionally I sense some pressure among Unitarian Universalists to make ourselves appear to be indistinguishable from the Presbyterians, the Methodists, the Baptists, or the Congregationalists. Why do we exist if we want to be just like, or if we are similar enough, to Presbyterians, Congregationalists, and Baptists—whatever? Why do we persist in some separate identification?

I believe we persist because the differences are very important. One difference has to do with human freedom and human decision making. Where, and under what circumstances, do we believe that prayer is useful, and where, and how much, do we believe that we are responsible for our own behavior and for each other's behavior as human beings? Where do we leave off, and where does the Divine take over? Do we allow the Divine to take over in our lives, and in what ways do we refer to the Divine?

The great message of our Judaic-Christian tradition, especially in the creation stories of the Old Testament, is that we are free to choose. The way that we Unitarian Universalists have often interpreted this, however, is that we are free to think whatever we want to think. And we can, and often do, spend a lot of time thinking about offbeat ideas and we can spend a lot of time talking about them here.

My point, however, is that it doesn't make a damn bit of difference to anybody what you think about or what you talk about here, if you don't do anything about it.

Our interpretation of the Biblical message and of what we have learned from life today is that I am responsible for my life and you are responsible for your life. Religion helps us to relate to our own lives and to each other, so that we can make thoughtful, responsible decisions.

Unlike the traditional Orthodox Christian interpretation of decision-making, we can make responsible, rational decisions. If we refuse to make such decisions, then we are indeed sinners, but sinners in a very different sense than traditional Christianity defines them.

The challenge to us, then, in living our faith, is to really make it a different faith— to make it different by using our freedom to make responsible decisions and to take responsibility for them. We, ourselves, have the power and the responsibility.

Our religion helps us to shore each other up, to say to each other, "You can decide". There are times when each of us is down, when we need help and assistance in affirming that we do have the power, we do have the information and we do have the ability and the strength and the courage to carry on! That's one of the values our religion brings to us.

Our challenge is to work on the issue of what will make a difference in the days and years ahead. And we're open to doing that.

But it isn't something that we can just lie back and say "Well, I'm a Unitarian Universalist principally because I like the freedom of speech and the freedom of thought that exists" and then not do something with these freedoms. The world needs more from us today than just our enjoyment in the self-indulgence of free thought in the church. The world desperately needs people who are thinking about the future and saying, "We need new insights. We need new vitalization of ourselves, new vitalization rather than re-vitalization, new vitalization of life on different premises with different comprehensions and different understandings than those we've gotten along with up to now."

We can no longer afford the luxury of a world in which everybody thinks we're all sinners and that Humanism is some evil, social phenomenon that must be stamped out. We can't remain silent and wait for our critics to go away, and hope that the controversy over Humanism will fade. Our critics won't go away, unless more and more people stand up to them and say, "You're wrong."

It's only through the existence of Humanism in the last 1500 years that we have the civilization we have had and which remains today. And if we don't get to work on preserving that civilization and expanding it, we are, indeed, all lost.

We need hope for ourselves and for each other, and we must share the message of Humanism, because the world certainly needs it now.

If we really want to change the way things are going in the world, all of us will need to do more than just pray about it. We need to support each other, diverse as our opinions may be, on what to do and how to do it. It is important that we share a freedom of environment in which we can change and exchange ideas, and in which we can find ways of working together to effect some improvement in this world.

That's why we're here, and that's why I am a Unitarian Universalist minister. It's also why I think the difference between us and the conventional Christian denominations is very important, and I say Vive la Difference!

[**Editor's Note**: A poem *Mountain Impasse* by John Updike, American writer, 1932-2009, was removed from the original manuscript (as a Related Reading) because of copyright guidelines. However, it is possible to access this poem on the internet to read or purchase in its entirety, if you so desire.]

The Devil: Myth or Monster

The traditional explanation, in our Western-tradition culture, as to why we do things that we don't want to do or why events happen in the world which we don't want to have happen is because *it's the work of the Devil!*

Satan or the Devil has probably come to seem like a pretty silly idea to most of us today. But I think we owe it to ourselves on occasion to ask ourselves: are we really better or happier as human beings for having identified this idea of *the Devil* as a mythological idea and therefore false and so much excess intellectual baggage? Are we really better or happier for having disposed of this explanation for evil as meaningless?

It's interesting, in tracing the development of this theme, that nowhere in the Old Testament of the Bible does Satan appear clearly personified until the very late books, the Book of Job, for instance. The Old Testament religion which is, to a large extent, the religion that has been maintained by Judaism, is not what we would call a dualistic religion. (A dualistic religion considers there are two forces at work in the world, a good force opposed by an evil force.) However, the Old Testament views life as potentially good and that if life fails to be meaningful and to be viable it is the fault of man's infidelity to God. The Old Testament view sees no division of forces, a good force versus an evil force. It is man, evil man, opposed to God.

The idea of a two-power universe, which we know in Christianity and which is widely expressed in the New Testament, is a concept that, as well as historians and scholars can determine, we inherited from the Persians. Friedrich Nietzsche's [German philosopher, 1844–1904] great book, *Beyond Good and Evil*, is based in part on the interpretation of the Persian's idea of a dualistic world.

In this religion, which is now almost extinct except for a small, very elite group of well-to-do people called the Parsee who live in India, God is viewed as living in opposition and under threat of the devil. At a later point, this idea was preempted and incorporated into Christianity and into Mohammedanism, or the religion of Islam. Prior to that time, this dualistic concept does not seem to have been part of the intellectual equipment of humanity.

Christus Stendhal, Swedish Lutheran theologian and an American citizen, delivered a paper, *Apostle Paul and the Introspective Conscience of the West*, at Harvard's Roman Catholic-Protestant Colloquium in 1963, then published in 1964 as part of a collection, *The Ecumenical Dialogue at Harvard*. Stendhal's paper poses the thesis that it is to Martin Luther (1483–1546), rather than to Paul (50 A.D), that we should look for the development of the idea that the Devil is personally after us as individuals; and that we should feel guilty for being so hard on Paul. Stendhal's point is that as we read Paul our eyes and ears and hearts are heavily influenced by the thoughts of Martin Luther and by those of Sigmund Freud.

It is to Luther that the strong sense of the demonic, as applied to personal individuals, certainly can be attributed in our culture and in our society.

For 1200 years prior to Luther's time, there wasn't nearly as much stress placed (except in certain exclusive monastic orders) on the rightness of one's individual conscience. Not even the idea of conscience was developed until about 400 years ago. Conscience was not viewed as a special capacity that one had to develop for oneself.

Nevertheless, the idea of the devil was certainly conceived in both the Old Testament and the New Testament as being in some sense *psychological,* but mostly in the sense of a creator of mental illness. Many of the miracles in the New Testament, for example, refer to a person who was seized by the devil and therefore had epilepsy, or was born lame, or could not speak coherently. Part of the function of a responsible religious leader was to exorcise devils from people.

And we have our own word *demented*, which comes from the word *dementia*, to indicate someone who has been seized by the devil. We have less and less, emphasized or thought about—or have been willing to talk about—the demonic or the devil in our lives.

One of the principal tenets of early Unitarianism was to reject the idea of predestination or election. Predestination or election means that God had figured out before he created the world who was *destined* to get saved and who wasn't, who was going to lead a healthy life and who was going to lead a sickly life, who was going to be poor and who was going to be rich, and ultimately which people were going to heaven and the rest be damned. (Imagine, he had this all figured out!)

Well, both the Unitarians and the Universalists rejected the idea of predestination and, in the rejection of this idea, opened the way for further reflection of any idea of the existence of a devil.

Their viewpoint was further reinforced by the work of' the great Viennese psychoanalyst, Sigmund Freud, who postulated that much of the teachings of Christianity, as interpreted in Victorian society, provoke a kind of guilt in people which makes them ill, either physically, mentally or both. And the function, then, of psychoanalysis in its early forms was seen to be the exorcism of *guilt*, rather than the exorcism of *devils*. The function of the psychoanalyst often was, and continues to be, to reassure people that they shouldn't feel guilty about various thoughts or actions and to assure them that they have learned to feel guilty either through family life, church or societal influences.

It is, however, a puzzling and difficult problem of our time that—as we have trained ourselves to feel less and less guilty—we have developed more and more people who feel that life is meaningless, pointless or hopeless. In exorcising the guilt in people, in wiping out the potentiality for feeling guilt about various behaviors, more and more people in our time tend to express themselves as feeling that life is simply meaningless. Surely, we must raise the question: are we better off with or without feelings of guilt?

There's an old saying that unfortunately always strikes me as being exceedingly true. That is, that a New Englander was asked "What is the difference between Universalists and Unitarians before we merged in 1961?" The New Englander answered, "Universalists believe that God is too good to send anyone to eternal damnation in hell and Unitarians believe that they're too damned good for God to send to hell."

And this, I think, is something that we carry over, all of us, somewhat into our personal lives. This manifests itself in our notion that *perfection* is possible for our self, for others, for our church, for our family, for our society.

We certainly should not constantly be making ourselves feel guilty about doing less than a perfect job about everything that we undertake. Let's do the best we can but let's accept that everything isn't absolutely perfect day in, day out; week in, week out; month in, month out.

I recently had a long and meaningful talk with the current head of our Department of Ministry in Boston, Dr. Joseph Barth. In keeping with the subject of the demonic, how to cope with it, and what stands in our way, he said to me, "You know, the best is the worst enemy of the better."

Perfectionism often keeps us from making steady meaningful improvement day by day. We are so busy comparing ourselves to the perfect example that we are dissatisfied with everything we do in the present and therefore never make much meaningful improvement.

Whether the devil is a myth or a monster created by guilt, feelings of meaninglessness, or by anxious urges to be absolutely perfect, it is essential to recognize that the best motivation in life is not fear, nor is the best motivation that of *guilt*.

The best motivation in life is that which we get when we see our capacities as they really are. Then we can progress in our lives with each other, with our families and friends. We can bring to our lives and our work a creative zest, wanting to be the best that we possibly can be – even as we know we are far from perfect.

Dick at his desk annotating a book for future reference.

Considering Visions of Reality in the New Century

The Dawn of Hope
On Creative Religion
Calm and Free
A New Life for All
Love: God's Presence among Us
Life is all Risks
Looking to the 21ˢᵗ Century
Sacred Texts

The Dawn of Hope

The dawn of hope, I believe, depends upon a creative religion of doing. If that religion is to be usable and effective, it must be comprised of a variety of elements which I will discuss in turn.

Religion must also provide or enable us to perceive a vision for ourselves. The account of Abraham [Genesis 12] tells how he went out of Ur, with a sense of acting in accordance with God's will and the belief that doing so would result in a better perception of the best relationship for all people everywhere in the world.

By insisting on the recognition of and acknowledgment of reality, and our limitations within it, we affirm the most essential element in our recognition of God and the ultimate good. We courageously affirm that, when more of us honestly hold the mirror up to ourselves and see ourselves as we really are, a new day for all will surely dawn—a day when true rationality, tested by God's reality in the world, will triumph. That is our nameless vision.

Religion, too, must help us to sustain and develop our vision in the face of disappointments, long delays, and adversity.

We need patience and staying-power, the capacity to tolerate ambiguity, confusion, and delay. Religion must constantly correct our personal perception of our individual vision, and help to differentiate it from mere self-seeking.

In our own time, we have been faced with, and continue to be faced with, conflicting claims that *systems* alone will completely solve our problems. For example, we have the various systems of communism. A few years ago, we had the systems of fascism. In our own country, we have those who claim that an 18th century system designed for an unsettled and largely rural country should be preserved, unmodified, and if possible, imposed even by force everywhere, regardless of the circumstances and needs because, it is thought, it is in our self-interest to preserve that system intact.

The parallels of an 18th century system with that of the Biblical Northern Israelites is so striking, that it hardly seems necessary to point out that it is beset with all of the calamitous dangers inherent in confusing our own vision with our own immediate self-seeking interests.

Religion must provide the dynamics to free those individuals who need to be freed to enable them to act constructively for the realization of that vision. Here we can think of Paul, Luther, and Freud as such individuals.

We have rejected the highly emotional *conversion* experience and are attempting to replace it with the cultivation of the capacity for creative, responsive and innovative behavior. Certainly it is true that not all people— perhaps not even most people—need *conversion* experiences. Our success with our particular educational approach remains to be demonstrated, however.

The gist of the social gospel, as a repudiation of the centuries-old self-image of Christianity that the primary end of humanity was to be found in Heaven, came from the Old Testament.

Religion also must provide us with useful principles—as different from rigid systems, sets of rules or rote, ritualistic procedures—which will help us to discern with reasonable confidence the most appropriate action in each situation of life in which we find ourselves.

All of these components are interlocking and interdependent, and our religion—any religion—runs the risk of becoming dangerously irrelevant if it emphasizes only one or two at the expense of the others.

The great Unitarian and American statesman, Adlai E. Stevenson [1900–1965], said: "This must be the context of our thinking—the context of human interdependence in the face of the vast new dimensions of our science and our discovery. Just as Europe could never again be the old closed-in community after the voyages of Columbus, we can never again be a squabbling band of nations before the awful majesty of outer space."

Stevenson's greatness is attributed to his profound faith in human potentiality, despite a realistic evaluation of our nature and all of our weaknesses, especially our infinite capacity for self-deception.

We are encouraged to expect the dawn of hope again. Our brightest hopes dawn only when we have faced our meanest actions and our most humiliating failures. Only then, with candid realism, do we begin to build truly and surely for the future. It is this kind of doing which religion must inspire.

Utopia is to society what hope is to the individual. Utopia and hope are visions of reality that come ahead of time

~

Related Reading

Faith gives substance to our hopes, and makes us certain of realities we do not see. It is for their faith that the men of old stand on record. By faith we perceive that the universe was fashioned by the word of God, so that the visible came forth from the invisible.

—*Hebrews 11:1–3 NEB*

Religion must lead us to commit ourselves by our concrete actions to the realization of our vision—at least in part—in the here and now."

––Walter Rauschenbush, American clergyman and author,
Religion and the Social Order, **1861–1918**

*Charles Redd of Urban League with Ruth Langhinrichs
at Unitarian Universalist General Assembly*

On Creative Religion

One needs to clarify what is actually meant, or what can possibly be meant, by the term *creative religion*. The word *creative* has been extensively used, by our elected and appointed associational leaders, and by our thinkers, our theologians, philosophers and ministers for a number of years.

Perhaps the most influential and responsible use of the adjective *creative* has been that of our venerable philosopher-theologian, Henry Nelson Wieman, who coined the phrase *creative interchange* in the 1930s. Creative interchange, in his view, is the highest human experience. It is the cultivation of a way of living in which, through the completely open interplay between human beings and their environment, they self-consciously (and progressively) create original experiences for themselves. To Wieman, the cultivation of creative interchange is the function of religion, and the experience of creative interchange is the ultimate religious experience.

Wieman's thought has had a constructive influence on contemporary theology far beyond the limits of our Unitarian Universalist Association and we are all, directly or indirectly, deeply indebted to him for the contribution he has made to religion.

Our general usage of the word *creative*, however, reflects that many of us have somewhat different things in mind from those of Henry Nelson Wieman's definition.

To some Unitarian Universalists, *creative* means aesthetic worship—with beauty the central value. To others, it means the cultivation of intellectual novelty—experimentation emphasizing the avant garde. In this view, the function of the Unitarian Universalist church is to keep in the vanguard of thought, always to be intellectually ahead of the rest of the world. Others of our denomination concentrate on the religious education program and attempt to make of it an antidote for the stultifying and conforming tendencies of regular school experiences.

Each of these emphases has contributed to the vitality of our religious movement, and I anticipate and hope that they will continue to do so. But it seems important to recognize that each of them must always be kept in a subsidiary role. Primarily, by *creative religion* we must mean—and we must continue to mean—the development and practice of religion that leads each of us, members and friends, to the responsible, resourceful and satisfying living of life. We cannot afford to mean anything else. We must distinguish four characteristics of a resourceful creative human being:

First, such a person has sustained or regained a childlike freedom for spontaneous action and emotional responses.

Second, this person has sufficient confidence to experiment, to explore, to pioneer and to live at the frontier of all of his or her own capacities.

Third, such a person is free to enter into a variety of meaningful personal relationships without having predetermined desires, wishes or goals for the other parties involved. Such a person is always ready, in such relationships, to allow for the unpredictable to come into play.

Finally, the creative person is totally committed to the best, the highest values he or she can discern for humanity, for community, for family, for self, and is willing to make extensive sacrifices, if necessary, to help to bring these values to realization.

It is the challenge of creative religion to help its members to realize these potentialities. Arthur Koestler, in his brilliant book *The Act of Creation*, acknowledges that we have no precise, scientific ideas about how creativity can be cultivated, but he methodically presents all of the evidence about the phenomenon presently available to us, thus setting the stage for possible research which might follow. Koestler differentiated three domains of creativity, "Humor, which is related to feelings of aggression; discovery, dependent upon emotional detachment and rationality; and poetic, the aesthetic or artistic, which is inspired by positive emotions." Koestler's observations of the fluidity of the boundaries between science and art are especially pertinent: "There are no frontiers where the realm of science ends and that of art begins; and the universal man of the Renaissance was a citizen of both." So, also, our universal religion is a domain in which the aesthetic and the scientific views of the world must have free interplay with each other. Koestler's point is of particular importance to us as we attempt to define and understand creative religion: that the creative process is always the same in one respect; that it consists in the discovery of hidden similarities. The decisive turning points in history are discoveries which uncover what has always been there.

These discoveries may come after a period of cultural breakdown and anarchy; in parallel (in several different places at the same time); as a result of cross-fertilization between the seemingly distant provinces of science and art; and from widely separated places and times. The constant factor in each of these approaches to discovery is that they all are ultimately dependent upon the scientist or the artist possessing a profound and sophisticated awareness of humanity's past. In our search for new and better ways for people to live together, we are ultimately faced with a question of recognition: how do we know something is new, original, better?

When are we living in creative freedom? How do we know? The answer is clear: we live in creative freedom only when we are familiar with, when we understand and when we can make the best possible use of our past—both personal and collective—of all humanity in history. The whole idea of creativity is unthinkable—either artistic and scientific creativity or the concepts of responsive living and creative religion—unless our personal and collective past is used as a constant referent and resource. True freedom is, in large measure, our freedom to use our past constructively and resourcefully in the present.

A. S. Neill, founder of Summerhill, a modern experimental school in Suffolk, England, established in 1921, maintained that *freedom works*. Neill believed in the potential of the child to love life and that the aim of education and of life is to work joyfully and find happiness. Summerhill does not offer religious education but focuses on basic humanistic values. Neill states, "The battle is not between believers in theology and nonbelievers in theology; it is between believers in human freedom and believers in the suppression of human freedom: When a new religion comes, it will refute the idea of man being born in sin. A new religion will praise God by making men happy."

Neill and Koestler, between them, suggest three principles for responsive living, the goal of creative religion: First, we need to give one another—insofar as we are able—unstinted love, which means support, encouragement, and acceptance. Second, this love should lead us to help one another, to help us make decisions about ourselves and the kind of world in which we live, and to act on them. Third, love can only be given and decisions can only be made responsibly when we are able to make the fullest possible use of our individual pasts and of the past, the history of all humanity. Innovations which are not fully grounded in the past are mere novelties and thus, ultimately deceptions or delusions.

In our Unitarian past, one of our most creative innovators was Theodore Parker. Parker, who was born in 1810 near Lexington, Massachusetts, educated himself by reading so widely and with such comprehension that he succeeded in gaining admission to the Harvard Divinity School in the 1830s without formal preparation. There he was soon put to work, to help earn his way, teaching Hebrew, a language which he had mostly taught himself. When, in 1842, Parker initiated his reform of Unitarian orthodoxy, he came equipped with the creative love and deep knowledge of our history, as Neill and Koestler described. Parker, no matter how pressed for time, was noted throughout his life for the limitless resources of love which he had accessible for those who came to him in various kinds of troubles and needs. Parker was rarely, if ever, at a loss to make responsible and resourceful decisions which profoundly shaped the creative contribution of his own life to his ideal of a universal religion which was socially responsible—responsible to the problems of slavery, poverty, war, woman's rights and innumerable others.

Parker, when he died, left to the city of Boston his personal library of 15,000 volumes; they became the core of what we now know as the Boston Public Library. He is reported to have digested the contents of them all so well that he could discuss them meaningfully without referring to them. Parker took his dependence on the past seriously.

Theodore Parker's hero was Martin Luther. Both of these men loved and revered the apostle Paul, for it was Paul who caught a vision of the universal potentiality of Christianity. Theodore Parker learned from the past, from Martin Luther and from Paul, that responsibility and responsiveness are impossible when a person gives ultimate loyalty to the conventions of the world to the law. But once a person has grasped his or her new freedom, it becomes possible to observe the useful laws with love and to work to reform the others. As Koestler says, The creative act…the revolutionary contribution, is both destructive and constructive."

The prize about which Paul speaks in the letter to the Corinthians is immortality:

> All the runners at the stadium are trying to win but only one of them gets the prize. You must run in the same way, meaning to win. All the fighters at the games go into strict training; they do this just to win a wreath that will wither away, but we do it for a wreath that will never wither. *1 Corinthians 9:24-25 JB*

Paul, of course, did achieve immortality—an immortality of a sort which he never imagined. His immortality fell to him because of the fresh, frank, provocative way in which he expressed himself in his letters after he had found himself as a man.

The prize, which Unitarian Universalists desire, is the kind of inner freedom and resourcefulness which Paul, Martin Luther and Theodore Parker exemplify. Helping each of us to achieve this prize in some way for ourselves should be the goal of a truly creative religion. And religion, to be truly creative, must be in continuous, profound dialogue with the past.

Related Reading

The salvation of mankind lies only in making everything the concern of all.

**—Aleksandr Solzhenitsyn, Soviet writer,
1970 Nobel Prize, 1918–2008**

Calm and Free

Mysticism is natural. Engulfing us in this incredible universe is the sense of being one with nature. Mysticism is the sense of being human, the fulfillment of awareness, receiving others unto ourselves. Our experience is holy if it is human.

In *The Common Experience*, jointly authored by J. M. Cohen and E. F. Phipps in 1979, the Hindu philosopher Krishnamurti resolutely refuses to regard himself as a teacher. He holds that there is no need for any special practice or instruction in meditation. He says:

> There is nowhere to go if you do not seek to travel, you're there already. Meditation is a never-ending moment. You can never say that you're meditating or set aside a period for meditation. It isn't at your command. Its benediction doesn't come to you because you lead a systematized life or follow a particular routine or morality. It comes only when your heart is really opened. It comes only when you're not there at all and its bliss has no continuity.

And, in *Mystics and Zen Masters,* Thomas Merton wrote:

> The basic aim of religion arises out of human experience itself, the experience of suffering. And it seeks to provide a realistic answer to man's most urgent question, how to cope with suffering. The problem of human suffering is insoluble as long as we are prevented by our collective and individual illusions from getting directly to grips with suffering in its very root within ourselves... Piercing the illusions in ourselves that divide us from others must enable us to obtain solidarity with our own brothers and sisters. With openness, compassion endowed with secret resources of creativity, this love can transform the world. Only love can do this.

We associate the word *spiritual* with calmness and freedom. What does the word *spiritual* mean? The word *spiritual* relates to, consists of, having the nature of spirit. It's not tangible, it's not material. It's of, or concerned with, or has something affecting the soul, whatever we may think that means. The spiritual is something that is of, from or pertaining to God. It is sacred, of or belonging to a church or religion—something that is ecclesiastical. And let's not forget, of course, that spiritual is what we call the folk songs that our black brothers and sisters have created for religious music over the years.

We can't really understand what spiritual is without talking about spirit, the word on which it's based and from which it derives its significance. To me, spirit—that which is traditionally believed to be the vital principal or the animating force in human beings—is what spirituality is all about. Spirituality is a way of behaving, of relating to each other, of gathering together so that the vital, principal or animating force of our human lives, together and separately, receive their full expression. Spirituality, which develops and enhances and sustains the human spirit, is something that has vigor, vitality and significance to us.

Spirituality, as it relates to being calm and free, is not antimony or an opposite. Spirituality is not an either—or kind of word. There are churches that are spiritual and there are churches that are socially oriented. And never the twain shall meet, according to this way of thinking, a narrow simplistic view.

People also define spiritual as doing something by oneself. As long ago as Jesus' *Sermon on the Mount*, which advises people not to make a public show of their divinity and prayer life, as long as there has been religion, there has been this tension between our impulse to be spiritual, to get in better touch with the vital forces of our lives, and between doing so in solitude or doing so in the company with others. I think we need to do both.

Calmness and freedom are not necessarily perfect, nor is this a state that any human being is able to sustain all the time. The English poet, John Donne, [1572–1631] wrote this about serenity four centuries ago:

> A memory of yesterday's pleasures, a fear of tomorrow's dangers, a
> straw unto my knee, a noise in mine ear, a light in mine eye, and
> anything and nothing of fancy a shimmer in my brain troubles me

in prayer, in meditation. So, certainly there is nothing in spiritual things which is perfect in this world.

Donne is affirming an experience that almost all of us have had of mind-wandering, of being preoccupied. How well and how often can we focus our intensity and our search for vitality without having our minds wander off in a variety of directions? Be reassured, say I, everybody has that problem for a long, long time!

Calmness and freedom is a state of being in harmony, in harmony with life, of relating harmoniously to the world in which we find ourselves and allowing that world to enhance, to stabilize and to strengthen us for the problems of life.

We must practice believing. Even in the somewhat sad, negative note at the end of Ranier Maria Rilke's [the German poet, 1875–1926] *Ninth Elegy,* the affirmation is there—life will go on, we will come through:

> Not because happiness really exists, that premature prophet of imminent loss, not out of curiosity, not just to practice the heart, it could still be there in laurel, but because being here, being alive, amounts to so much. Because all this here and now, so fleeting, seems to require us and strangely concerns us: us, the most fleeting of all, just once, everything, only for once, us, here, now.

Enjoy it. Grab it: in calmness and in freedom.

New Life for All

In his book *Psychology and Its Social Needs* written in 1953, Ira Progoff, an American psychologist, who has taken a decidedly different path from most of his contemporaries, had this to say when he wrote about his connection with the Swiss psychiatrist Carl Jung in the 1950s:

> To the extent that an individual in any society is able to identify his psychic energy with an established system of meaning and belief and is able to experience a psychologically true but corresponding religious symbol, he is safe from neurosis.
>
> He gives up his individuality and receives the psychic security of social value. In this regard, the difference between modern civilizations and other civilizations is merely that it is more difficult for an individual to find a satisfying belief to which to identify himself in any society.
>
> When he seeks to transcend the beliefs which are socially true or accepted and to integrate into his personality universals, the pre-condition is necessarily a regression and, therefore, a neurosis.
>
> The literature of the world and, especially of religion, is filled with symbols of the psychic process involved in this search. It is expressed in the story of how Buddha foreswore his secure position in society and withdrew into solitude to receive his message; and again in the event of Christ being tempted by the devil. The concept of rebirth is an especially strong symbol; for example, in the Christian religion, its meaning is that one can have new life, can be born again, if one believes in Christ... Rebirth is thus acquired through this symbol [which is] in psychological terms, a psyche—rebirth.

All religions celebrate new or renewed life. The spring equinox is at its essential core a universal religious observance and one of our most ancient and basic religious affirmations. Everywhere it is related to new or renewed life.

There is hope for the downtrodden; there is hope for the dispossessed; there is hope for the slave. There is a new, better way, to find spiritual harmony with life than the ones which we are presently relying upon.

Examples could be given from other religions of the world as well. But, instead, I prefer to pursue the question: why do we feel that we need a new life? Many of us left behind some form of orthodoxy; this was for us an affirmation that we were undertaking a new religious life, a new orientation to the universe, a new orientation in relationship to other human beings. Why, then, do we need renewal?

We do need a *new* or *renewed* life. Carl Jung and many others have been aware for more than fifty years of the collapse in values of Western Civilization. From the ten years preceding the outbreak of World War I to the present, there has been a disintegration of traditional religious symbols; there has been disintegration of traditional moral values; there has been a disintegration of the conventional family; and there has been a disintegration of most of the cultural integrative forces.

Human beings living in Western Europe or the Americas feel very much adrift. With the collapse of values has come a collapse of the significance of the symbols. There are two ways to respond to this. One is to hold on to the old, whether or not it has any meaning beyond a nostalgic, sentimental one, because it makes us feel good to have something to hang onto. This stance is comprehensible. No matter how liberated and freedom-affirming we may be, every one of us wants to have some people, some values and some principles which we can trust, on which we can depend in tumultuous times like those we are living through at present. Inevitably, some people will turn back to a simple, irrelevant faith because it seems the only path to a sense of security. For one reason or another, Unitarian Universalists refuse this option of a reaffirmation of a rigid outmoded orthodoxy. We also have rejected the so-called middle-of-the-road Christian stance in which everything is watered down, where the old beliefs are outwardly affirmed, if inwardly questioned. We dislike the hypocrisy of that.

The second way we may respond is to set ourselves on paths that enjoin us to be open about what we do believe as well as about what we don't believe. Beyond that, we have made a commitment that most of us find difficult to live up to much of the time. That is a commitment in this time of turmoil, of changing collapsing values, of devaluation of traditional religious symbols, to work our way through, to strive, to fight toward a new faith that is relevant and meaningful to human beings today. We are here to find ways of affirming life, of seeking a deeper spiritual life, of finding meaning for ourselves, and meaning for the society in which we live that will set our new lives on a more harmonious path.

That is the challenge which continues to drive us and the one that, like Peter in the garden with Jesus, we deny at times, two times, three times, many times, because like the leadership of Moses, like the leadership of Jesus, like the leadership of Buddha, developing a new, deeper spiritual life is hard. It is painful; it takes work; it takes energy; and, as Progoff noted in the writings of Carl Jung, it involves turning ourselves back on an old lifestyle, risking something he calls neurosis, to go through a stage of feeling deeply out of harmony with oneself and perhaps with the society in which one lives, before bringing through some new, deeper, more fulfilling meaning.

The symbolism of Moses' life, Buddha's life, Jesus' life is that they persevered to do all that they could when most of us give up. Our message is to renew our commitments, not just to move away from orthodox religion that is no longer adequate for the era in which we are living. We must stand forth and persevere with the difficult work of finding new, deeper, more significant meanings and values for the world in which we are living.

Gathered together, it isn't all bad and it isn't all difficult. Life can be joyous and fun, a delight, and I hope that aspect of life is yours as much as the challenge which all of us need to hear.

Related Reading

To the great problem of our century— the lack of a belief in the meaning of life, the experience of emptiness, of hopelessness, of despair—the suggested description of man's basic nature gives an answer: life is accepted if meaning in the midst of meaninglessness is accepted. The experience of meaninglessness, emptiness and despair is not neurotic or psychotic only if the power of affirmation of life in terms of 'in spite of' has vanished. The negative elements are possible consequences of man's basic nature, or finite freedom. They are universally real, but they are not structurally necessary. They can be conquered by the presence of a healing power.

—Paul Johannes Tillich, the *Portable Dragon*, 1886–1965

Love: God's Presence among Us

I want to share something with you that I love from the book *Locked In,* by James Moody Gustafson, the American, Christian ethics writer, who writes:

> All my life I lived in a coconut. Isn't that a great place to live? It was cramped. It was dark, especially in the morning when I had to shave. But what pained me most was that I had no way to get in touch with the outside world. If no one out there happened to find the coconut and crack it open, then I was doomed to lead my whole life in a coconut. Maybe even die there. I died in that coconut. A couple of years later, they found me shrunk and crumbled inside. "What a shame," they said. "If only we had found it earlier, then maybe we could have saved him. Maybe there are more locked in like he is." And they went around and they cracked all the coconuts within reach, but it was no use. It was meaningless. It was a waste of time. A person who chooses to live in a coconut, such a nut, is one in a million. But you know, I couldn't tell them because I was dead, that I have a brother-in-law who lives in an acorn.

Let's not live in coconuts. Let's not live in acorns. There is a world to be appreciated. There are fantastic things to be seen, to be felt, to be desired, to be aimed toward and to be achieved. You are an incredible gift. You were never meant to spend your life in an acorn or in a coconut. The greatest sin would be to experience less than your capabilities.

In *Souls on Fire* by Elie Wiesel, naturalized American novelist, historian and social activist, there is this beautiful statement: "When you die and go to meet your maker, you're not going to be asked why you didn't become the Messiah, or why you didn't find the ultimate cure for cancer. All you're going to be asked is why didn't you become you. Why didn't you become all that you had the potential of being?"

It is very important for us to understand far more fully what love has meant in other people's lives, what love may mean in our lives, what the potentialities of love are. Love is a very paradoxical matter; and I think there are three significant paradoxes of love.

There is this growing aspect of our lives of building the walls around ourselves higher and higher. The higher we build the walls and the more emphasis we put on them, it seems, the more we provoke people into trying to find ways to circumvent them! We all know how this happens with our children. Aren't the matters we make the most fuss about—the ones we make prohibitive and off-limits, if we're not very careful—aren't those things the very ones they are most likely to become entranced with and to persevere to seek ways to find how to get involved in them? This is one of the paradoxes of being a loving parent, isn't it?

The second paradox is one that abounds in our world and confuses us. On the one hand, we have been through a whole era and this man, Leo Buscaglia, the American educator and author, 1924–1998, has persevered and survived the era and is still proclaiming the message of "Jump in and love other people." His message was much promoted in the '60s and early '70s even though some people misused it, misunderstood the message or found it didn't work very well for them.

So that we have, on one hand, the message that we open ourselves up, love everybody who comes into your life until they prove that they're not worth it, assume that they're to be trusted. And the other message that runs contrary to this is to maintain separateness from other people. Our fundamental religious message and belief is that a person is a part of you and you are a part of that person. And there are qualities in that person that are your qualities. Maybe the very reason that you and I despise that person so much is because there are some things about that person that epitomize the worst impulses that you and I have on occasion. All of these feelings are feelings that are directed against ourselves very often, our suspicion that if we aren't very careful, this too will happen to us—and there is some reality to that. So, the alternative approach is to be very careful about separating ourselves from others in the sense of being clear that we understand that each person is discreetly different from us.

There is also a positive message and it's very much prevalent today that, in order to love other people, you have to understand how different from yourself they are. Not how much alike they are, but how different from you they are. Again, this is a kind of paradox that can't be fully resolved because we ought to be recognizing that the worst people whom we can think of have characteristics in common with us. They have human potentialities that need to be opened up and awakened, that love from us and from others can help to bring about and transform. And at the same time, we have to recognize also, that in some very significant ways, others are discreet and different from us. The message from many persons, from biblical sources and from non-biblical sources, is that through loving, we encourage people to discover and to embody in their lives the best that is in themselves—which is not the best that's in you.

Finally, the third paradox is that of affirmation of people. We have two messages about how we deal with love and one is always to give affirmative messages to other people. We're advised to begin by affirming those things that are positive, which is a good way of making you think of the constructive characteristics of that person.

Nonetheless, contrary to this, we have another whole set of advice (that all of us are saddled with and, especially in a Calvinistic style of religion), and that is that we should constantly be challenging others to be the very best that they're able to be. If you aren't critical of the way other people behave, they're never going to change and improve. So the position to take with other people is that the most loving thing you can do for them is to constantly challenge them to do better than they presently are.

Now, those two things are clearly in conflict with each other. It's difficult, if not downright hypocritical, at one and the same time to say, "Gee, I love you for the way you smile and the way your mind works; and I think it's despicable the way you fail to do this, this and this when it's so evident that is what you *ought* to be doing. And the only way you're ever going to grow is to change."

M. Scott Peck, the American psychiatrist wrote in *The Road Less Traveled* (1978) that one of the mysterious natures of love is that no one has ever arrived at a truly satisfactory definition. Peck wrote: "In order to explain it, therefore, love has been divided into various categories—Eros, filial, agape, perfect love, imperfect love, and so on. So, anyone who gives one definition of love is being somewhat preposterous and is doomed to failure, no matter what."

Having said all these things about love, it is very clear that the human enterprise will either flourish or fail on the basis of how much trust there is, how much affirmation, how much respect for each other as discreet individuals, and how much recognition there is that every person in his or her discreetness is somehow very intimately related as one human being to another.

The message of many myths of the childhood—of Jesus and his birth, of the myths of the birth of Buddha, of a world of stories about children and childhood—is that there is love in the world; that love can be very powerful, that it is multifaceted and that it is full of paradoxes and challenges. Still it is central to our function as human beings.

[During this sermon on Love, clarifying that love extends beyond just humanism, Dick stopped mid-sentence to check on the well-being of a small bird that had the misfortune to fly against the window pane of the sanctuary. Once assured that the bird was not seriously injured, Dick resumed.]

∿

Related Readings

At every moment you choose yourself. But do you choose yourself? Body and soul contain a thousand possibilities out of which you can build many I's. But in only one of them is there a congruence of the elector and the elected. Only one—which you will never find until you have excluded all those superficial and fleeting possibilities of being and doing with which you toy, out of curiosity or wonder or greed, and which hinder you from casting anchor in the experience of the mystery of life, and the consciousness of the talent entrusted to you which is your I.

—Dag Hammarskjold, *Markings*, published posthumously

I may speak in tongues of men or of angels, but if I am without love, I am a sounding gong or a clanging cymbal. I may have the gift of prophecy, and know every hidden truth; I may have faith strong enough to move mountains; but if I have no love, I am nothing. Love is patient; love is kind and envies no one. Love is never boastful, nor conceited, nor rude; never selfish, nor quick to take offense. Love keeps no score of wrongs; does not gloat over other sins, but delights in the truth. There is nothing love cannot face; there is no limit to its faith, its hope, and its endurance. Love will never come to an end. In a word, there are three things that last forever: faith, hope, and love; but the greatest of them all is love.

—*1 Corinthians 13 NEB*

A quotation from Jack Paar [American TV personality], who said: "My life seems like one long obstacle course with me as the chief obstacle."

—**Leo Buscaglia's *Living, Loving, and Learning***

Life is all Risks

I do believe that, occasionally, history makes some extraordinary claims or demands of a few people. It doesn't, for the most part, make heavy demands on the lives that most of us are destined to live. That, however, doesn't mean that life isn't risks or that it isn't important.

However, to say, as my title suggests, that life is all risks is to create a redundancy in saying the same thing over twice, tending to make the word *risky* meaningless. If you say life equals risks and risks equal lives, then you only need one. You're saying zero equals zero and you don't need two of the same thing. You call it one thing or the other.

It's like the old argument and eventual refutation of much of what's called religious pantheism. The extreme religion, pantheism, says God is everywhere. God is in sticks and stones, and light bulbs and banners, and plants and buildings, and walls and chairs and tables. Well, if that's the case, then you really don't have any need for God. If everything is God, then it's not a very significant term.

We're looking very often in life for ways to discriminate, to differentiate ourselves from the normal. And, one of the words we use is *risky* to describe certain situations, certain character traits or certain lifestyles. Some are even more risky than others!

Risks are part of being alive, of being a human being. The first and most obvious one is birth. We could go on through the various events of life. Childhood is a time in which there are indeed many risks. Health epidemics, accidents, natural disasters, earthquakes, avalanches, floods—are all risks of which we've had some experience. Then we have war and all the other human-contrived disasters. And let's not forget interpersonal relationships. They can be very risky. Establishing meaningful relationships with other human beings is often not a simple, straightforward task. And finally, there's another kind of risk that we're very much aware of today. Some days don't you begin to wonder what is really safe to do? What is safe to eat? What is safe to breathe? Where is it safe to live? The whole matter of degradation of the environment, pollution, contamination of various foods, and so on.

Life does have, in and of itself, certainly a multitude of risks. In addition, we could say, statistically, that the chance of each one of us, every single one of us, ever having been conceived and born, let alone surviving up to this moment is very slight. Far more potential lives have been lost along the way than the few of us who survived. So in some sense, we each have some reason to feel a little gratitude and pleasure about the fact that we're around to *smell the coffee*, as Ann Landers puts it, "There are an awful lot of folks out there who never got a crack at it." I think we also have to say, if we dwell on the risks, most of us would have a pretty uncomfortable time of our existences. We survive as human beings in no small part by fairly consciously pushing into the forgetful part of our brains, the part that allows us to ignore reality, the knowledge that all those risks are out there, or that we might never make it from bed to kitchen to make a pot of coffee.

I'm thinking about the riskiness of life in a somewhat different context, however. We live at the end of an era that was characterized by George Bernard Shaw, the great Irish playwright, as being one of middle-class morality. The restrictiveness of the English Victorian morality, middle-class morality, also dominated life throughout most of the United States for a fairly long time. The great homogenous, conforming middle class reached its apex or epitome of all that it stood for, both in terms of values and in terms of terrible dullness, in the 1950s.

Inevitably, some of us were led to rebel against restrictive Victorian morality in favor of individualism, often predicating this on their knowledge and awareness of our great Unitarian thinker of the 19ᵗʰ Century, Ralph Waldo Emerson. The rebellion, however, came into major force and the enjoining of us to take risks during the 1950s with the rediscovery of the works of the German philosopher and cultural critic, Friedrich Nietzsche (1844–1900), the Danish theologian, Soren Kierkegaard (1813–1855) and the French existentialist writers, Jean-Paul Sartre (1905–1980) and Albert Camus (1913–1960). The idea, the notion, that a human being was okay, that it might even be desirable or necessary to undertake or lead a risky existence on occasion, and that it takes some risk in life began to be championed in the public realm in the '60s.

Unitarian Universalist churches, paradoxically, are institutions established to protect the unique and non-conforming human beings in our society. Unique and non-conforming human beings, however, don't tend to want to associate themselves with institutions! And often, once into institutions, they play havoc with what happens to the institutions! On the one hand, our legitimate, obvious and desirable impulse is to stand up for unique individuals, to encourage such people to take some risks in life, to be a little more themselves, to do some things that they wouldn't have the courage and power to do on their own. On the other hand we need some kind of structure, some kind of institution, and some kind of place in which to do this. Don't we all have to sacrifice a little bit of our individuality and our uniqueness in order to keep this institution rolling along, and to meet certain demands for commitment that it makes on us?

We have idealized certain figures that we hold up as being the mentors of risk and they're very important to us in our religious tradition.

Sisyphus, rolling his rock up the hill, became one in the 1950s— although some people always found difficulty in that rather negative view of life that implies happiness consists of and persists despite all of the difficulties of life; and that most of life is rolling rocks up hills for no apparent good reason. Even if they tend not to stay when you get them up there, you're grateful for the opportunity to be alive and able to push the rocks. And that was perhaps the most negative kind of vision. [See *The Myth of Sisyphus*, Albert Camus, first American edition, 1955.]

More positive ones come from Socrates, the great individualist Greek philosopher of 3,000 years ago, who brought us, as did several other people, the concept of knowing thyself, and standing for what one believes even if it necessitates dying for it.

The figure of Jesus also played a very important part in this concept. For some of us, and for many people in our culture, Jesus, the non-conformist, came to be very much a part of theological and religious understanding during the 1960s.

Also, we have Michael Servetus, from the Reformation— a brilliant Spanish man [physician and theologian, 1511–1553], a loner with no circle of friends, who formed no church, no organization, who despite a whole lot of very good advice insisted on going to Geneva, Switzerland, where John Calvin was in control and on telling John Calvin that he was all wrong about the Doctrine of the Trinity. Calvin sent him away once and Servetus said, "I won't go away, you've got it wrong, I insist that you listen to me and change your teaching." Finally, Calvin felt his back was pushed to the wall, so he lit a great big bonfire and threw Servetus in. And nobody can say that Servetus wasn't warned. He had plenty of reason to know that he was offending somebody who had a tremendous amount of power and influence and who could not tolerate to be crossed. But Servetus elected to do that anyhow. Servetus had persisted for at least twenty years. He was pursued by the Inquisition after publishing books in 1531 and 1532 expressing his anti-Trinitarian views. Servetus changed his name and began medical studies in Paris in 1538. In 1546, Servetus sent Calvin parts of a draft of his latest work. Arrested by the Inquisition in 1553 for heresy, Servetus escaped and headed for Geneva. He was apprehended and condemned for his anti-Trinitarianism and opposition to infant baptism. Servetus was burned at the stake in October, 1553, near Geneva.

And rightfully, we see some mark of that which we aspire to be, affirm to be or want to celebrate in the individual when she or he knows a certain truth and is willing to stand up and insist on it to the authorities, even at the risk of one's personal life.

Then, to the 19th century figures, Ralph Waldo Emerson and, more explicitly, to Henry David Thoreau, who withdrew from human commerce and went and lived by a pond by himself. All these people have and continue to serve as inspiration to us to face life and life's risks.

I think that life is a risky business. Yes, life is full of some very natural and some not-so-natural risks. We do need to take risks, but risks for what, under what circumstances and for what results?

Related Reading

I wonder if the river...harbors a secret desire to flow north...if the stars envy the Earth? Teach us...to accept them.

—Excerpt from *Acknowledgment of Limitations,* by Burton D. Carley

[Editor's Note: This reading was reduced from the original manuscript because of copyright guidelines—which diminished its size and emotional impact. However, it is possible to access some or all of it on the internet to read or purchase in its entirety, if you so desire.]

Looking to the 21st Century

What is the future of religion? Can we shape the future? Should we try to do so? A half century ago, the Viennese psychoanalyst Sigmund Freud, in *The Future of an Illusion*, posited that as more and more human beings came to recognize that the sacred symbols and revered persons of religions are actually subjective projections of human wishes, needs and expectations, religion itself would be unmasked as a mass self-deception which should be allowed to wither away. Freud's view, coupled with Karl Marx's contention that *religion is an opiate of the masses* and under girded by Kierkegaard's, Feuerbach's and Nietzsche's devastating critiques of 19th Century Christianity, has carried much weight with educated persons ever since. [Soren Kierkegaard was a Danish philosopher who lived from 1813–1855. Ludwig Feuerbach lived from 1804–1872 and Friedrich Nietzsche from 1844–1904; both were German philosophers.]

Today, much of the earth's population lives with religious indifference, although, from time to time, a few are temporarily swept with zealous fervor by the debased, exploitative and fear-evoking views of an Oral Roberts, a Billy Graham or a Jerry Falwell.

Freud, et al, however, offered as a total view what proved to be a partial one. The mysterious power of life is far less defined by our human projections about it. For example, my own personhood—fully described by the various ministerial stereotypes which people carry with them—are projected on me from time to time!

We earthlings continue to need a fresh religious vision, a faith which includes, yet transcends, all known forms of Christianity, Buddhism, Hinduism, Islam, Humanism and other religions. This is the religious task for the future to which we Unitarian Universalists were called more than a century ago—and have largely neglected since, while dissipating our energies in various in-house parochial battles.

Newsweek's December 1990 cover story discussed the return of Americans, particularly those of the *baby-boomer* generation, to religion. The article reported that the changing needs and expectations of this generation, as they themselves have become parents, are leading them to return to the church. *Newsweek* expressed the opinion that: "The quintessential boomer church may be the Unitarian Universalist Association which emphasizes that each individual is the ultimate source of authority. Instead of an individual fitting a religion, it is a religion to fit the individual."

Far from *an opiate of the masses*, Unitarian Universalism does not offer simplistic answers to the complex questions of the masses, nor does it rely on symbolic projections to address the needs of the people. Unitarian Universalists continue to respond to human need—sociological, psychological and spiritual—and yes, we can shape our future.

~

Related Readings

Be an opener of doors for such as come after thee, and do not make the universe a blind alley.

—Ralph Waldo Emerson, American essayist, poet, philosopher, 1803–1882

I don't know who or what put the question, I don't know when it was put. I don't even remember answering, but at some moment I did answer *Yes* to someone or something. And from that hour, I was certain that existence is meaningful and that, therefore, my life and self-surrender had a goal. From that moment, I've known what it means not to look back and to take no thoughts for the morrow. I came to a time and place where I realized that the way leads to triumph which is a catastrophe, and to a catastrophe which is indeed a triumph. That the price for committing one's life would be reproach and that the only elevation possible to man lies in the depths of humiliation.

—Dag Hammarskjold, *Markings,* **Swedish Statesman, 1905–1961**

> We leave the here below
> And build beyond instead
> The land of the Great Yes

—Paul Klee, Swiss artist, 1879–1940

> Time is too slow for those who wait,
> Too swift for those who fear,
> Too long for those who grieve,
> Too short for those who live
> Time is eternity.
> The hours fly, flowers die.
> New days, new ways, passeth
> Love stays.

—Sundial Inscription, University of Virginia

Sacred Texts

[**Editor's Note:** In response to a request for the title of a book that changed his life, Rev. Langhinrichs wrote in 1982:

> *South Wind* by Norman Douglas profoundly affected me when I first read it more than forty years ago. It precipitated a change in my ethical beliefs. When I enrolled at Northwestern in 1938, my belief was that the distinction between right and wrong was always clearly distinguishable. Reading *South Wind* initiated a process of evaluation of this morally absolutistic position and my eventual rejection of it. *South Wind* is a brilliant work in many ways and delightfully amusing as well. I have enjoyed rereading it many times."

UU ministers are often asked what books are their sacred texts? The following is a list of such books—those marked with an asterisk (*) indicate works read by Dick when he conducted a discussion group in the South Pacific (as a lieutenant) during World War II:]

Adams, Dr. James Luther. *On Being Human Religously*
Adams, Dr. James Luther. *The Prophethood Of All Believers*
Allport, Gordon W. *The Individual and His Religion*
Altheizer, Thomas. *The Death of God*
Barth, Karl. *The Word of God; The Word of Man, The Bible, etc.*
Baum, L Frank. *The Wizard of Oz*
Becker, Ernest. *The Denial of Death*
Becker, Ernest. *The Structure of Evil*

Bellows, Saul. *More Die of Heartbreak*
Breasted, James. *The Dawn of Conscience*
Bronowski, Jacob. *The Ascent of Man*
Brownell, Baker. *Art is Action*
Buber, Martin. *A Believing Humanism*
Buber, Martin. *The Ten Rungs: Hasadic Sayings*
*Bunyan, John. *Pilgrim's Progress*
Burke, James. *The Day the Universe Changed*
Buscaglia, Leo. *Living, Loving and Learning*
*Carroll, Lewis. *Alice in Wonderland*
Camus, Albert. *The Myth of Sisyphus*
Camus, Albert. *Reflections on the Guillotine*
Cervantes. *Don Ouixote*
Cohen, J. M. and E. F. Phipps. *The Common Experience*
Connolly, Cyril. *The Unquiet Grave*
Cousins, Norman *The Celebration of Life*
Cox, Harvey. *The Secular City.*
Cox, Harvey. *The Feast of Fools*
Descartes, Rene. *Meditations*
Didion, Joan. *Slouching Toward Bethlehem*
Deikman, Arthur J. *The Observing Self, Mysticism, and Psychotherapy*
*Douglas, Norman. *South Wind*
Eliot, T. S. *The Cocktail Party*
Erikson, Erik H. *Gandhi's Truth*
Fletcher, Joseph. *Situation Ethics*
Frankl, Viktor. *From Death-Camp to Existentialism*
*Franklin, Benjamin. *Life and Letters of Franklin*
Freud, Sigmund. *The Future of an Illusion*
Fromm, Erich. *Escape From Freedom*
Fromm, Erich. *The Revolution of Hope*
Fowler, James W. *Stages of Faith*
*Galsworthy, John. *End of Chapter*
*Goethe, Johann Wolfgang *Faust*
Goodman, Paul. *Growing Up Absurd*

Gould, Stephen Jay. *Time's Arrow, Time's Cycle*
Halberstam, David. *The Reckoning*
Hammarskjöld, Dag. *Markings*
Hanh, Thich Nhat. *The Miracle of Mindfulness!*
Hawking, Stephen W. *A Brief History of Time*
Heller, Joseph. *God Knows*
Helverson, Ralph N. *Living In The Questions*
Hofstadter, Douglas. *Godel, Escher, Bach*
Hofstadter, Douglas and Daniel Dennett. *The Mind's I*
James, William. *The Will to Believe and Other Essays*
Kafka, Franz. *The Metamorphosis*
Kaufmann, Walter. *Existentialism from Dostoevski to Sartre*
Kaufmann, Walter. *Religion from Tolstoy to Camus*
Keillor, Garrison. *A Prairie Home Companion*
Koestler, Arthur. *The Act of Creation*
Kundera, Milan. *The Unbearable Lightness of Being*
Kushner, Harold S., Rabbi. *When Bad Things Happen to Good People*
L'Engle, Madeleine. *Two-Part Invention*
L'Engle, Madeleine. *Walking on Water*
Macquarrie, John. *Existentialism*
Malraux, Andre. *The Voices of Silence*
*Maugham, W. Somerset. *Of Human Bondage*
May, Rollo. *Love and Will*
Menninger, Karl. *Whatever Became of Sin?*
Merton, Thomas. *Mystics and Zen Masters*
Miller, Perry. *The Life of the Mind in America*
More, Sir Thomas. *Utopia*
Nelson, Carl. *Eternity Can Wait*
Niebuhr, R. Richard. *Radical Monotheism and Western Culture*
Nietzsche, Friedrich. *Beyond Good and Evil*
Pagels, Elaine. *Adam, Eve. and the Serpent*
Pagels, Elaine. *The Gnostic Gospels*
Polanyi, Michael. *Personal Knowledge*
Peck, M. Scott, M. D. *The Road Less Traveled*

Plato. *The Republic*
Progoff, Ira. *Jung's Psychology and Its Social Meaning*
Progoff, Ira. *The Dynamics of Hope*
Rauschenbusch, Walter. *Religion and the Social Order*
*Reves, Emery. *The Anatomy of Peace*
Rilke, Rainier Maria. *Duino Elegies*
Rilke, Rainier Maria. *Stories of God*
Robbins, Tom. *Another Roadside Attraction*
Rogers, Carl, *On Becoming a Person*
Royce, Josiah. *The Hope of the Great Community*
Salinger, J. D. *The Catcher in the Rye*
*Scott, Sir Walter. *Ivanhoe*
Siegel, Bernie S., M.D. *Love, Medicine, and Miracles*
Skinner, Clarence. *A Religion for Greatness*
Slater, Philip. *Pursuit of Loneliness*
Smith, Wilfred Cantrell. *The Meaning and End of Religion*
Smullyan, Raymond. *The Tao Is Silent*
Smullyan, Raymond. *This Book Needs No Title*
Terkel, Studs. *The Good War*
*Thurber, James. *The Middle-Aged Man on the Flying Trapeze*
TiRich, Paul. *Shaking of the Foundations*
Tillich, Paul. *The Eternal Now*
Tuchman, Barbara. *The March of Folly*
Viorst, Judith. *Necessary Losses*
Vonnegut, Jr., Kurt. *God Bless You, Mr. Rosewater*
Vonnegut, Jr., Kurt. *Slaughterhouse-Five*
Wagenknecht, Edward. *Utopia Americana*
Wakefield, Dan. *Returning*
Werfel, Franz. *Embezzled Heaven*
Wieman, Henry Nelson. *Man's Ultimate Commitment*
Wiesel, Elie. *Souls On Fire*
Wood, Barry. *The Only Freedom*
Wright, Conrad. *A Stream of Light*
Wright, Conrad. *Liberal Christians*

Zacharias, James L. *Letting Go and Having It All*

Zaehner, R. C. *The Comparison of Religions*

Versions of Bible:

ESV	English Standard Version
JB	Jerusalem Bible
KJV	King James Version
NEB	New English Bible

Part II

One Man's Legacy

Mid-Life Career Change

Early Efforts to Straighten Out the World
Religious Odyssey
Entering UU Ministry
Leaving Grosse Pointe Farms, Michigan for Harvard Divinity School
Strength to Say "Yes!"

Dick Langhinrichs at three in his
hometown of Rock Island, Illinois

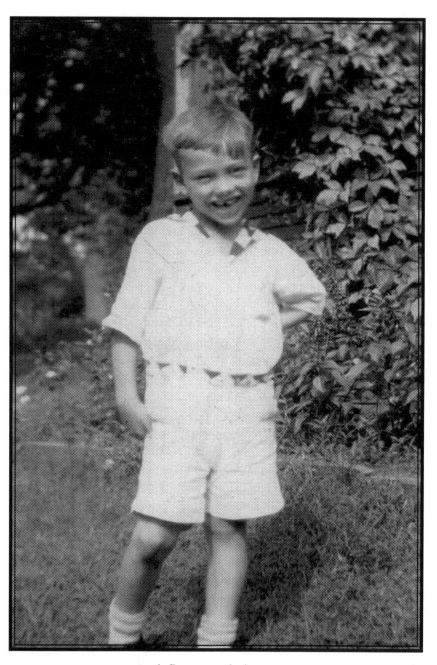

Dick flirting with the camera

Dick and his dog Blacky are playing in the yard,
perhaps thinking of heading to the river.

Dick at eighteen years old—a sophomore at
Northwestern University in Evanston, Illinois

Early Efforts to Straighten Out the World

I was born and raised in Rock Island, Illinois, a town on the Mississippi River. I graduated from Rock Island High School with an *A average*, was an officer of Hi–Y, the Blackhawk Tribe History Club and the Dramatic Club, won many inter-school prizes in oratory, debate and extemporaneous speaking, sang in and accompanied the Glee Club and appeared in class plays and operettas. My father was a butcher who owned his own business and from the age of twelve I worked for him part-time. After I reached fourteen, I supported myself each summer by working at the Rock Island YMCA camp.

In 1938 I was admitted to the Northwestern University School of Speech. There, in addition to my academic work, I was vice president of the Class of 1942, president of Theta Xi social fraternity, and an honor society member. To supplement scholarship funds awarded me, I waited tables at the Alpha Phi sorority, worked for an engineer in the N.U. Radio Department and was employed full time as a YMCA camp counselor during the summers.

Although we did not know each other there, Ruth and I attended Northwestern in some of the same years. Ruth studied journalism, English and philosophy on a full scholarship and graduated cum laude in 1944. She then went to New York and had a successful journalistic career with *Look, Scholastic,* and *Science Illustrated Magazine.* In 1952, she was appointed as Associate Editor on the *Ladies' Home Journal* in Philadelphia, where she specialized in young adult concerns.

I was discharged from the Marines on December 17, 1945, exactly three years to the day from when I enlisted. I decided to go to New York to write a novel. I was encouraged to do that by some of the guys who were in the Marine Corps with me. I went to New York to live the life of the Bohemian and write the great American novel about the war. This was great. Everybody had their priorities. I got the novel written and got an advance from Rinehard & Company. I couldn't get it revised to satisfy them. I ran out of money and ended up with a bleeding ulcer in the hospital. It was my first personal brush with death. I was hospitalized at St. Vincents for about a month. In those days they didn't know how to deal with bleeding ulcers, not that they have ever learned completely. I lost a lot of blood. That's the way things were.

Those were exciting days in New York. There were lots of Communists around. Lots of my friends were Communists. It turned out that guys that I had been friends with in the Marine Corps were Communists. When Henry Wallace ran for the presidency, I met Ruth, my future wife, who was a journalist but also an organizer for the Newspaper Guild. We were involved in all the radical causes that we could find to put our hands on to get the world straightened out after WWII. Her father had died when she was a child and she also had gone through Northwestern on scholarships. We were introduced through mutual Northwestern friends. We were friends for a long time. We didn't get married for another 13 years. We were very idealistic young people who also found life very interesting in New York City in those days, which it was. We lived in Greenwich Village. The Village in 1946–47 was a far safer place to live than Fort Wayne, Indiana is today.

—Richard Alan Langhinrichs, from his writings

Religious Odyssey

My mother was raised a Roman Catholic and educated in a Catholic orphanage in Dubuque, Iowa. She graduated from the eighth grade and went to work as one of the first telephone operators in Iowa. She eventually was transferred by way of Waterloo and Burlington to Davenport, Iowa where she met my father whose people had emigrated from Germany. My mother's people were among the early Irish settlers in Iowa. My father's people, by background, had been Lutheran. My parents met, dated and married in 1913 and because my mother had no close family connections and my father's mother and immediate family did not feel very well disposed toward Germans and the German-Lutheran Church, they decided they would be married in the Presbyterian Church. They traveled by inter-urban to Clinton, Iowa and were married there in the First Presbyterian Church. The first child born to them was a girl who died at birth, then a son who was born in 1915, and in 1921, an answer to my brother's persistent prayers for a little sister, my parents decided to have one more child, and I'm what they got. Within about a year of the time that I was born, my mother was involved in changing me and giving me a bath when the telephone rang. This was about 1922, still the early, early days of telephones. While she went to the telephone I picked up the talcum powder and apparently inhaled it. When my mother discovered that this had happened, she simultaneously or in very quick succession called the doctor who in those days made house calls and he came in a great rush to make sure that my lungs were okay. She then called the photographer because no official baby pictures had been taken and she called the Presbyterian minister and he came and baptized me. This all happened within a few hours of my inhaling the talcum powder. This was the beginning of my *Religious Odyssey*.

During my childhood we regularly attended the Presbyterian Church in Rock Island, Illinois. The minister was William G. Ogilvie and his wife Louise's religious influence on me was considerable. He was a follower of Harry Emerson Fosdick, a modernist and very liberal Presbyterian for the Midwest in those days. This was in the late 1920s, early 1930s. His wife Louise was a Quaker and very unconventional for that time and place. She made no pretense in being a Presbyterian and made no pretense, let alone of converting and joining the church because she was the minister's wife, which is not to say that she didn't fulfill her conventional roles that were expected of the spouses of male minsters in those days. She entertained people and presided at church suppers and did all that kind of stuff. But she made it very clear that she was a member of the Society of Friends, a Quaker, and had different religious views from her husband and that was tolerated by the congregation.

I was very active in that church all the way through high school and very active in the Hi-Y and the YMCA as well and grew up as a very super conforming high achieving youngster striving to do everything that my brother didn't. He never forgave me for being born at all let alone for being male. He still hasn't to this day. He's seventy-one and we have some difficulties in getting along with each other still. He did poorly in school, he set fires, he was in trouble with truant officers, he failed courses, he was prayed over a lot and my role was clear, it was an easy way to succeed to get all kinds of praise. I was able to conform quite readily and did it with a vengeance so that each year I would get into school, following my brother by four or five years, and the teacher who didn't know anything about our family would think "Oh my God, another Langhinrichs is here" and in about a week she would announce in front of our class "Richard is entirely different from his brother Lester. He's as different as day and night." This was a terrible burden for my brother to bear and at the time it seemed okay with me but looking back on it today it was not a very good message for a child growing up to hear. I went off to all the church's activities, helping with church conferences and in the summer that I was fifteen I decided to become a Presbyterian minister and arranged to join the church on Christmas Eve during a special ceremony. The minister took a great deal of interest in me, teaching me to play the piano and the organ and involving me in cultural activities. My mother was able to be supportive but my father was a butcher/meat cutter and worked 12–15 hour days, six days a week, every week. In those days, during the depression, his meat market would be open on Sunday mornings from 6:00 A.M. until 12 noon; a terrible and difficult life for someone who was a shopkeeper, especially that kind of a shopkeeper. He always managed to look after our family during these difficult and tough times but we somehow did as well as most people did in those days, and somewhat better.

I had every intention of going into the ministry when I graduated from high school to study for the Presbyterian ministry. Some classmates from Rock Island High School, two or three of them, had gone to Northwestern University. Conventionally in town they went to Augustana College or if they went away to school they went across into Iowa to the University of Iowa which was about forty miles away or down to Champaign/Urbana to the University of Illinois. I had a very bright Ph.D. English teacher who was quite radical for Rock Island High School. She graduated from the University of Chicago and she introduced me to reading such things as the poetry of Robinson Jeffers which had words like *fuck* and *shit* printed right on the pages and were available at the public library in Rock Island, Illinois. My mother did not read such books from the library and did not understand that a high school teacher would assign such books for me to read as a part of my education. Miss Pearson didn't feel that I was being sufficiently challenged by Ralph Waldo Emerson which was prescribed reading my senior year: she introduced Robinson Jeffers and some others as well. The themes of those poems in case you never read them was *incest*, a variety of fascinating topics for a sixteen-year-old male and things that totally mystified my mother who read everything that I read and worked hard at getting me educated. Miss Pearson tried to get me to go to the University of Chicago. There was a lot pressure from other people at high school not to apply there because it was communistic. This was 1937–38 but the students who were at a Northwestern rally persuaded me that I could get in there and find the money and scholarships; that I could go to Northwestern, and I believed them. I scraped around and played the games that I'd learned to play as a kid with my parents and ended up going to Northwestern.

Economically and socially, I really had no business being there and never fit in very well but I did it. As soon as I got to Northwestern I became an atheist. I did try the Presbyterian Church in Evanston before I began to be contaminated by freshman English. I was greeted at the door by a man in a morning coat and all the ushers wore morning coats. He asked me what I was doing there and I said I was a Presbyterian and a student at Northwestern. He replied that it was interesting and said that they didn't get students there very often. He then asked if I could wait there at the door and he excused himself. All the pews were owned in those days and I eventually figured out that the process he was going through was to find someone who would permit me to sit in his or her pew. They finally ushered me into their church. I don't know what the theology of the minister was but it certainly wasn't anything like Southpark Presbyterian Church in style and content. It was nothing like I'd been exposed to.

—Dick's delivery to the Ohio Valley Unitarian
Universalist Minister Association,
All Soul's Unitarian Church, December 8, 1986

*Dick chatting with his Aunt Florence and Ivan
Lebamoff, mayor of Fort Wayne, Indiana, (1972–76).*

Entering UU Ministry

[**Editor's Note:** To be an accredited UU minister, a man or woman first must be approved by the UUA's Ministerial Fellowship Committee. This is the body which appraises the credentials and abilities of prospective ministers. A candidate must have earned an undergraduate degree and a Master of Divinity degree or higher degree from an accredited theological seminary.

Specific ministerial training is offered at Starr King School for the Ministry in Berkeley, California; Meadeville Lombard Theological School in Chicago; and the Harvard Divinity School which ducats ministers from other denominations as well. However, a degree from any accredited school is acceptable provided the candidate has specific education in Unitarian Universalism.

—Settlement Handbook for Ministers and Congregation, Transition Office, Unitarian Universalist Association, January 30, 2013, and asides.]

I wished to become a Unitarian Universalist minister because I was not satisfied with the way I spent my time as a businessman. After some years in New York City, I accepted a position in Detroit. At that time, the psychologist who evaluated the screening test battery (which aided me in making my selection) warned me that while I would find the work challenging to begin with, it would not ultimately satisfy my needs as a concerned, mature human being—that it was improbable that any job in business could do so.

In Detroit, I committed myself to a variety of church and community affairs. I became special events chairman of the Friends of Modern Art of the Detroit Art Institute, a member of the University Club, a member of the Fine Arts Society (a Detroit amateur theatrical group), was chairman of the Citizens' Committee for the Detroit Adventure (a local cultural activity which has attracted considerable international publicity) and worked several years as a unit chairman for the Detroit United Foundation campaign.

During those years, I participated in many non-credit courses, seminars and discussion groups in semantics, philosophy, literature, architecture, industrial psychology, music, modern art, drawing, business ethics and French. One particular interest has been existentialism, and I have read much of the literature since first learning of it in 1942.

I became an active member of Grosse Pointe Unitarian Church (GPUC): my activities included leading worship service for the junior high group, planning and organizing the GPUC Sunday Evening Forum Series, leading the unmarried young adult group (under 40s) and effectively assisting in the GPUC successful building fund drive.

My decision to seek the B.D. degree at Harvard and become a Unitarian Universalist minister has evolved slowly but irrevocably. I have been motivated toward a vocation as a parish minister since high school days. Two of the strongest influences of my childhood were Dr. and Mrs. William G. Ogelvie, our Presbyterian pastor and his wife in Rock Island, Illinois. Dr. Ogelvie was a liberal religionist and his wife a Quaker; both were primarily interested in the practical, day-to-day results of religious belief. They encouraged me to enter the ministry, but I decided otherwise for two reasons: (1) I did not feel that I, personally, could function to my own satisfaction as a minister without direct experience of the kinds of life situations my parishioners would be facing; and (2) I could not reconcile either the Ogelvies' or my theology with the sanctimonious dogmatism of Presbyterianism. To me, the two were irreconcilable.

During the Second World War and for long afterwards, I questioned the relevance, if any, of the organized Christian church to our society, so I embarked on a career in business. But finally, through Unitarianism, I began to realize that pertinent responses of many of my doubts existed, that an honest approach to religious experience existed, and I acquired a vision of the potential strength of the church and a conviction that I must play a role in its evolution. A part time involvement, particularly with business demands always taking precedence, no longer satisfied me. Full time commitment is the only answer.

And so I have made this commitment. The effects of this decision to enter the Unitarian Universalist ministry have involved us in many difficulties; but I, with the generous, confident support of my wife, am most excited about the future.

—letter to Harvard Divinity School, 1962

Leaving Grosse Pointe Farms, Michigan for Harvard Divinity School

Dear Ms. Kreicker,

It may well be too late for you to be able to use this response to your request for materials bearing upon the life of Dick Langhinrichs. I have been trying to press to completion the preparation of my own book, and have been neglecting too much else in so doing. If the material below is too late, or too wide of the mark, I will certainly understand.

I was, alas, not very close to Dick's orbit after he got into his ministerial career. What I experienced most directly was the period just preceding his entry into Harvard Divinity School, and the time of his entry into the Fort Wayne pastorate. I have checked my copies of the Grosse Pointe Church newsletters and Sunday bulletins of that era, which enable me to write the statement below with confidence that the details are on the mark.

I was Minister of Grosse Pointe (Michigan) Unitarian Church when Dick and Ruth Langhinrichs first visited, and soon thereafter joined our congregation. They were two of thirty-two new members welcomed into membership on November 15, 1959. As we got acquainted, Dick's restless dissatisfaction with his life in the business world was soon evident, and then his growing determination to do something about it. I knew of his studies and experience in literature, speech and drama; and for a while had the impression he might move toward teaching in the academic world.

In the *Grosse Pointe Unitarian*, Volume XI, Number 23, dated February 21, 1961, Edith Hakken's column, *Who's Who At GPU?* in which Dick and Ruth were profiled.

Dick's initial inquiry about the path one would follow to become a Unitarian minister came as no great surprise. I was glad to be able to supply the needed information, and sincere in encouraging his interest. The next thing I knew, he had chosen Harvard Divinity School, had applied for, and had secured, admission. All too soon Grosse Pointe would be losing him and his family to Cambridge.

On June 10, 1962—shortly before his departure for Harvard—Dick participated with me in the Grosse Pointe Sunday Service. I introduced him with these words:

> I have asked Dick Langhinrichs to participate with me in the service today for the very special reason that, as you know, he is shortly to enter Harvard Divinity School to prepare for the Unitarian ministry...Much as we shall miss Dick and Ruth and their two little girls, we are at the same time very proud to send forth from this Church another candidate for the liberal ministry; and we honor and respect them for the decision they have made. We know well that it has not been easy to do. It has taken courage to start. It will take vision and commitment to see it through. But these are virtues which we are satisfied that they are bringing to this undertaking. Dick, Ruth, we hope that you will go East thinking of Grosse Pointe Unitarian Church as your *home* church. It is the first Unitarian church to which you have belonged; and it is the church in which you made your decision for the ministry.
>
> Dick, I am sure that all of your friends and acquaintances in this congregation join me now in extending to you and to Ruth, our very best wishes for a rewarding period of study and preparation, and a fruitful ministry.

Inasmuch as it was the *closing Sunday* of the church *season* with *summer recess* beginning immediately, my sermon topic was *Making Recreation Creative*. Dick's contribution to the service was a series of four readings, selected by him, which spoke in one way and another to that sermon theme, and showed how he would operate in one important phase of the pulpit ministry. His readings were from: Clarence B. Randall, Lionel Trilling, and Mark Twain.

There is one more section to add to my part in Dick's story. In 1964, I left the Grosse Pointe Church to become district executive of the

Michigan-Ohio Valley District of the Unitarian Universalist Association, with its office in Fort Wayne, Indiana. One of the priority duties of my new position was to counsel ministerial search committees of the churches in my district; and one of the first congregations to require that particular service was the one *in my own back yard*—Fort Wayne! As a new resident of the community, I was about to *sign in* as a member of that church when, lo, their search committee took serious interest in a brand new Harvard graduate—Richard Langhinrichs! To avoid any appearance of conflict of interest, I backed off and waited to join until that question was settled.

I was, of course, delighted with the ultimate decision of the search committee and the congregation. At the close of the congregational meeting which elected Dick as minister, I went straight to the membership chairman, asked for the membership book, and signed it—thus becoming the first new member of the Fort Wayne Congregation under Dick's ministry! He had been a member of *my* church. Now I was a member of *his*! What a happy kind of turn-about!

—Letter from Rev. William D. Hammond 1992

Strength to Say "Yes!"

"When I'd mention religion, they'd smile shyly, change the subject then rush me outside."

"In our church, we hadn't even the standards of membership of a Kiwanis Club."

"So I concluded—after three years in the ministry—to quit, believing that if I stayed, I'd waste my life in directing a mutual-admiration society."

These were the captions over an article entitled *Why I Quit the Ministry* in the *Saturday Evening Post* (November 17, 1962.) While they may seem provocative to some and shocking to others, the article's revelations and this anonymous minister's response to his experiences are symptomatic of a larger problem faced by many orthodox churches. And we, as Unitarian Universalists, are not completely free from all of the problems this former minister encountered.

This *Saturday Evening Post* article, while specifically an indictment of a particular suburban Presbyterian church somewhere in the eastern United States—purporting to be an indictment of all American Protestantism in general—raises some significant questions for us in the liberal church.

To summarize, the Reverend Mr. Anonymous Clergyman reports the following:

- That a man and his opinions are no longer held in sacrosanct regard either by a congregation or a community just because he is a minister...or that his opinions are subjected to particular scrutiny, perhaps to downright suspicion, if he is known to be a clergyman;

- That most church members are either disinterested in or antagonistic toward the ideas of the authority of the church as an institution, of the Bible as infallible sacred scripture and of the traditional dogma of Christianity;
- That producing changes in a church is difficult, particularly if one attempts it through the methods currently taught in some *classical theological seminaries.*
- Therefore, that it would be better for him to quit the ministry, study sociology, then make life count by taking Christianity into the mainstream of life...to become a university professor able to influence young minds. Then sometime, perhaps, he would have a chance to enter public service.

Some may say that this analysis is regrettably accurate. But I strongly question whether the Reverend Mr. Anonymous Clergyman's church, or many similar churches, are *outside the mainstream of life.* Instead, I believe that its laymen have pretty well worked the church right into the stream—and that it is only some seminaries and their professors, some dogmatic theologians, some church leaders and some ministers who have kept themselves behind on an arid shore. By the writer's own description of the reported behavior of his congregation's members, life was swirling all around. His problem was that he was totally unequipped to cope with it.

One friend of mine, an educator, is especially thunderstruck at the prospect of this man's move from one area about which he is dangerously naïve, the church, into another about which his insight seems equally lacking, the university—in the vain hope that he will find there a place for himself and his form of Christianity. In a university he plans to mold young minds! And beyond that, he *hopes* to enter public service. Envision the future encounters of this man with our world! It is too appalling to speculate about for long.

Many of the outwardly conventional churches in America today are undoubtedly closer to the world as it is than some of their own leaders or some of us religious liberals would like to think. And this pragmatic proximity, despite the hand-wringing of their more pietistic ministers, may well save their churches rather than ruin them.

The churches of Christian Europe—Protestant and Catholic alike—stand empty on Sundays, monuments to what some churchmen term *Post-Christian Age*. Neither ritualistic liturgy nor brilliant, learned sermons by themselves interest many people.

Yet, here in the United States, the church as an organization—however secularized—is still very much alive. Perhaps this is because it is secularized! Suburbia, with its church bridge marathons, progressive dinners, bowling leagues and socials and square dancing, just possibly saves the Orthodox Church in America from a fate similar to that which it is experiencing in Europe.

In most American suburbs today, it is unnecessary to be active in a church. To belong, probably *yes,* to be active, *no.* And, outside the church, there are limitless opportunities for participating and leadership in such activities as bridge, eating, bowling and dancing. In addition, there ae golf clubs, yacht clubs and riding clubs for those so inclined. One can study astronomy, learn to speak French, act at the community theater or lead the Boy Scouts. No one has to be active in a church. Business and social promotions come just as fast if one is not. In general, life is simpler. Yet, many people choose to be active in the church. Let us think about this for a moment...Why?

Many of the human beings whom we most esteem have arrived at the kind of relationship to life which Swedish statesman Dag Hammarskjold (1905–1961; secretary general of the United Nations 1953–61) discovered in the mystics. In his journal, *Markings*, which was published posthumously, he wrote:

> They had found the strength to say *Yes* to every demand which the needs of their neighbors made them face, and to say *Yes* also to every fate life had in store for them when they followed the call of duty as they understood it.

There are gathering signs that some ministers are setting aside their preconceived notions of divinely revealed doctrine, or irrefutable church dogma, and their belief in a divinely imposed obligation to inculcate these beliefs and practices in church members. These ministers in orthodox churches are attempting to understand the world today—not as it was two thousand years ago—and to formulate a program for serving its needs and modifying its evil.

We, as religious liberals, must beware of smugly or self-righteously assuming that only we are being objective about the church in the world today. In many churches, a new kind of minister is emerging—men and women who are finding the strength to say *yes* to life.

Even with the Reverend Mr. Anonymous Clergyman's church, I will wager, one would find some outstanding people, men and women who distinguish themselves for their contribution to their congregational life, to their community life, to the schools of their community—persons making fine contributions to the world. You are probably familiar with the book *From Death-Camp to Existentialism.* It is an account of how a psychiatrist, Viktor E. Frankl, worked out a meaningful relationship to life for himself and his fellow prisoners while expecting death in a Jewish extermination camp in Nazi Germany. Fortunately, he survived to bring a whole new insight to psychiatric treatment and to report on his experiences in a concentration camp. Among other things, he says:

> We had to learn that it did not really matter what we expected from life, but rather what life expected from us. We needed to stop asking about the meaning of life, and instead to think of ourselves as those who were being questioned by life—daily and hourly. Our answer must consist, not in talk and meditation, but in right action and in right conduct. Life ultimately means taking the responsibility to find the right answer to its problems and to fulfill the tasks which it constantly sets for each individual.

I challenge the Reverend Mr. Anonymous Clergyman to set aside his preconceptions long enough to ask what life expects from him, and then with open eyes, to look again at his cast-off suburban church. I wonder if he might not find something like this:

- Some people who are troubled, anxious, scared and close to being defeated by life.
- A corps of people in his church who, while they cannot relate to his structured, sectarian theology, are proceeding to carry on important work for that church.

- A large number of members who have moved so far away from the traditional theological applications of the authority of the church and the Bible that a sensible conversation between a *classically trained* minister and them is no longer possible.
- Even larger numbers of people who remain outside any church, having legitimately found the church to be incomprehensibly unrelated to anything they know from personal experience, and who have rather courageously assumed full responsibility for their own spiritual and moral lives.

The churches of our Unitarian Universalist Association have always focused on the needs of people. Some ministers and many laymen in almost every denomination are increasingly, in their various ways, moving into the struggle with us. We should welcome them, for the job is larger than we alone can undertake. We should encourage them at every opportunity, for the church is still very much needed in the world today.

Our practice of religion holds forth a promise of personal strength and commitment. Our religion binds us to the responsibility to face life, to attempt to find solutions to its problems and to fulfill the tasks which it constantly sets for each of us. At its best, it gives each one the strength to say *Yes*. Let us willingly share that promise with all men and women wherever we find them.

—Dick's first sermon as student at the Harvard Divinity School, First Parish, Cambridge, MA, November 25, 1962

[Editor's Note: A poem *Love is a Place* by e. e. cummings American writer and painter [1894-1962], had to be removed from the original manuscript (as a Related Reading) because of copyright guidelines. However, it is possible to access this poem on the internet to read or purchase in its entirety, if you so desire.]

Impact on the Family

Ruth Langhinrichs with daughters at Harvard
in Cambridge, Massachusetts 1963

Julie and Jenny Langhinrichs in 1963
during Dick's years at Harvard

Early Life at Harvard

This Christmas season we discover: that bells and pull-toy caterpillars can be made from empty egg cartons; that Santa Claus and the Sandman are brothers; and that it is regretfully impossible for us to remember, by individual note, all the dear people we feel close to because last Spring Dick resigned his job to complete plans to enter the Harvard Divinity School as a candidate for the B.D. program and the Unitarian ministry (a decision he had been contemplating for two years.)

We arrived in Cambridge in June (leaving behind an unsold home, our household furnishings, and all but forty pounds of clothing. In July, Dick began a summer school crash program in Greek. The class met three evenings a week, three hours an evening. After four classes, the students were reading the New Testament in the original. During the day, Dick was a consultant for Pilgrim Laundry in Boston. Jenny cut her first tooth; Julie fell in love with a fire engine; Ruth pursued job leads and met Dick every Tuesday afternoon for a series of lectures on Contemporary Philosophy.

The summer streaked by. Dick passed the tough final with flying colors; Ruth became a consultant-writer and editor for Arthur D. Little Company. (She is currently working on an automation study.) Weary now of the gypsy life and the sub-let apartment, we were ready to settle, this fall, into the then available graduate student housing: a three-bedroom house with a wood-burning fireplace.

Classes began—all four of them. So did Dick's field work at First Parish Church of Cambridge (Unitarian), the meetinghouse where the presidents of Harvard worshipped since 1636. As student assistant minister he reads the lesson several services a year, delivers three of his own sermons, conducts the worship service for the junior church, and acts as an adviser to the Harvard-Radcliffe student group.

Jenny was one in October; Julie three, and Lucky ten in November. Dick delivered his first sermon, *The Strength to Say Yes*, in response to the *Saturday Evening Post* article, *Why I Quit the Ministry*. A fine, fine job and one much favorably commented upon.

And because the benediction from that service increases, for us, in meaning with the approaching New Year, we'd like to share it with you,

"May the faith that makes faithful, the hope that endures, and the love that triumphs, be with us always."

—Lovingly, the Langhinrichs

Arrival in Fort Wayne, Indiana

[**Editor's Note:** *The Protocol of the Call to UU Parish Ministry*:

Once a congregation has decided to seek a minister and a minister has decided to seek a congregation a very specific search process begins. Each prepares an informational packet. The congregation selects a search committee; the Board of the congregation appoints a negotiating team to prepare a draft of the ministry agreement into which the congregation and minister will eventually enter. The candidate will assess his or her worth and try to prepare for having their professional and even personal history examined in detail!]

The role of the UUA is to provide a list of approved prospective ministers to the Search Committee which then screens, interviews and makes its recommendation to the membership. The candidate then visits the congregation for a two-Sunday candidating week. (Since the congregation traditionally invites the candidate's spouse/and family, this week can be grueling for them too!)

At the end of the week the congregation votes on a motion by the search committee to call the minister on the terms proposed; if the call is sufficiently strong, and is accepted, the ministry begins as specified in the agreement. Most candidates hope for a vote of at least 95 percent; the Transition Office of the UUA usually discourages ministers from accepting a vote of less than 90 percent.

—Settlement Handbook for Ministers and
Congregation, Transition Office,
Unitarian Universalist Association,
January 30, 2013 and asides.]

We left the Ohio Turnpike and drove south through Bryan, Ohio. It was past 10 PM on Sunday, August 1 (1965), and we had been underway since early morning: Ruth, Julie, Jenny, Lucky (our dog), three goldfish, eight snails, our *indispensable* luggage plus boxes of miscellaneous things left over after the movers had driven away from our house in Cambridge—and me! Although our trip had been repeatedly slowed during the day by intermittent and heavy rain squalls, we passed two motels where we held reservations. Ruth and I were too excited to sleep comfortably until we were actually in Fort Wayne.

Beyond Bryan, we struck open country. Only occasionally did a car pass us headed in the other direction. The girls and Lucky were sound asleep. The night was particularly dark, damp, and silent. Ruth and I rode for several miles without speaking. Finally she murmured, "You really couldn't explain to anyone just what this is like."

Ruth implied many things by her remark: nostalgia, anticipation, anxiety, mixed and inexpressible emotions about the past and the future. But specifically she was referring to one particular aspect of the character of Fort Wayne which had most impressed us when we were here in June, an aspect that we both believed we had been unsuccessful in describing to our friends in Massachusetts when we returned there to pack and move. Repeatedly we had been asked, "Just where is Fort Wayne? What is it near?"

There is no easy way to answer such a question for someone unfamiliar with this part of the country. Fort Wayne, despite its location within convenient motoring distance of a number of large metropolitan areas, is essentially not *near* anywhere. It is where it is, set off from any other large urban area. And, it seems to me, this geographical fact has contributed immeasurably to the character of this community.

In New England, in the South, in the West and elsewhere in the Midwest, of course, there are other sizable communities which, like Fort Wayne, are geographically independent of any large metropolitan complex. I have visited many of them. All too often, life in such communities is vitiated by a destructive provincialism which permeates the atmosphere. It is also true, of course, that Chicago, New York, Rome and Paris—all are characterized by their individual kinds of provincialism as well. No community, large or small, is free of *provincialism* and so, I presume, Fort Wayne, too, has its own special brand.

But Fort Wayne's particular geographical location—surrounded as it is by great expanses of farms in every direction—seems to have contributed to an intense and largely constructive vitality, a vitality of cultural, economic and social life. This vitality is most impressive to us as newcomers to this community, as it must be to anyone who pays an extended visit here.

It is this positive, creative and challenging aspect of Fort Wayne that, as your new minister, I believe Unitarian Universalism is particularly qualified to serve, to support and—when appropriate—to criticize constructively. This past week a milkman, a gas company serviceman, a Lutheran saleswoman in a shop on Rudisill, a Jewish office worker and a Protestant minister have all spoken to me in glowing terms about our church and the constructive roles our members play in the life of Fort Wayne. Some of them even named some of you by name to me as outstanding citizens of this community! It seems clear that you have made your presence as a religious group in this community recognized and appreciated in a significant way. I am proud to have been called to be associated with you.

Last evening the board and many of your committee chairs met to make plans for the forthcoming church year. Details of those plans are reported elsewhere in this newsletter, and will be expanded in subsequent issues as these plans go forward. It is my hope and intention to work with the Board—and with each of you—to bring these plans to fruition in such a way that our church will move towards a healthy growth in membership and towards a much-needed fiscal stability during the coming months. This, I know, will require hard work from me—and from each of you. But I profoundly believe that the cause is worth the effort it will require.

This church, like Fort Wayne itself, is not very *near* anywhere else. In one sense it exists pretty much by itself, geographically at some distance from any other influential church of our association. That very fact can lead us to our own kind of provincialism—a withdrawn, negative sectarian— on the other hand, however, it can inspire us to a further demonstration of our capacity to be a vital, constructive force for good in the religious, social, cultural and economic life of Fort Wayne. It is my hope and intention to help to lead in the latter direction.

—Dick's first *Minister's Column*, UU Congregation of Fort Wayne Newsletter, Aug 10, 1965

*Unitarian Universalist Congregation
Sanctuary in Fort Wayne, Indiana*

Fort Wayne in the Age of Aquarius

My husband, Richard (Dick) and our daughters, Julie and Jenny, then ages five and three, made our home in Fort Wayne as the ministerial family and members of the Fort Wayne Unitarian Universalist Congregation in June, 1965, leaving behind us the academic community of Harvard where Dick, in a midlife career change, studied for the Unitarian Universalist ministry and served as an assistant minister at First Parish Unitarian Church of Cambridge, Massachusetts, responsible for UU students attending Harvard, Radcliffe or MIT. First Parish Unitarian Church, for those not familiar with it, is a historical wooden gothic church with a steeple, boxed and named pews, red carpet and two pulpits.

When I saw the Fort Wayne Meetinghouse with its swooping, winged, almost sassy roof, bright red doors and glass walls glittering in the bright sun on a June morning, I wondered how it was possible to meditate there, or even to follow the trails of a sermon with the delightful distractions of the singing birds and green foliage outside, visible through the multicolored stained glass behind the pulpit. So different from the generations of solemnity implied in both the exterior and interior of First Parish!

I can still recall the first severe winter Sunday morning of that first year. Because there was no carpet on the floors, no thermal window panes, the Meetinghouse was cold. Because there was no landscaping to block the bright sun that flooded the stained glass panels in the nave, it was difficult to focus on the speaker. I can still see a woman, bravely sitting in the first row of chairs in her overcoat, wearing fur-lined boots and sun glasses. Furthermore, she was sitting, as we all were, in a straight-back (folding) chair padded with a slippery, hunter green vinyl cushion.

Unlike First Parish, there was no choir, or organist (only recorded music). There was no name tag board, no director of Religious Education (RE) and only volunteers to help in the office. There was no dishwasher to hide dirty coffee cups and no janitor to empty the ashtrays. No paved parking and no sidewalks. Room dividers, not walls, separated all the various RE classes in the Social Hall and did nothing to muffle the noise of children.

We've come a long way since 1965. The architecture and facilities of our previous First Parish church and our new Fort Wayne church home may have been vastly different—and so were the communities—but the people and their principles were the same. In 1961, the merger of the Universalists and the Unitarians was completed and renamed the Unitarian Universalist Association (UUA). Rev. Dana McLean Greeley, minister of Arlington Street Church in Boston, was elected as the first president of the UUA. Actually, the first groups to merge were the two young people's group (the American Unitarian Youth and the Universalist Youth Fellowship), which were dissolved and replaced by the Liberal Religious Youth in 1953, eight years prior to the UUA itself.

In the long history of the Unitarian and Universalist movements, the application of religious truths to social problems has always been an important concern. Rev. Greeley wrote in the preface to *The Free Church in a Changing World*, "Liberal religion is not an institution; it is a movement in history, a set of values, and a way of life." [A compilation of the Reports of the Commission to the Churches and Fellowships of the Unitarian Universalist Association published by Beacon Press in a 1963 report by the Commission on Appraisal]

We were all living in the Age of the Aquarius, the era of the 1960s, an era dominated by war, assassinations and race riots. The 60's were the third straight decade dominated by war. We had lived through World War II, the Korean War (the undeclared so-called police action enforcing the role of the United States in protecting democracy around the globe) and finally Vietnam (fought in a country few could find on a world map). The civil rights movement, the woman's movement and President Johnson's war on poverty were also part of the 60's, as was police brutality in Chicago, and the race riots in Cleveland, Detroit and Newark, and series of shootings of leaders associated with the civil rights movement: President John F. Kennedy (1963); Malcom X (1965); Dr. Martin Luther King (1968); and Robert Kennedy (1968).

It was an era of heart transplants, space exploration, hippie communities, student uprisings and police brutality—as well as *Funny Girls, Odd Couples* and *Midnight Cowboy*. As children sang of being born free, their flower parents sang of wanting to hold hands. This was an era of transition, change and oscillation between Aretha Franklin's soul music and the hard rock of Jim Hendrix, between the man in the gray flannel suit and the hippie, between feeling good about your human potential and making big bucks.

So what were we doing at the Unitarian Universalist meetinghouse in the 60s to apply religious truths to social problems? How did we respond to the assassinations of leaders, the Vietnam War, the civil rights movement, the woman's movement, as well as the *Commission on Appraisal*? How did we cope and at the same time cultivate our own garden (as our own Ralph Waldo Emerson advised us)? How did we keep a roof over our meetinghouse, furbish our beautiful building, just four-years old in 1965? We did it the way UU's always do: we worked and played well together and we worked well alone and we worked well in still other groups; and if there wasn't anyone doing what needed to be done, we formed a group, headed the group, financed the group and kept it going until...it was no longer needed.

Margaret Mead defined an ideal community as one that has a place for each human gift. Mary Pipher, Ph.D., psychologist and author, expands this definition in her book *Another Country*. She wrote:

> An ideal community somehow keeps the best of the old ways and adds the best of the new. In it, there is a mixing of races, generations and viewpoints that enjoy the intellectual and cultural stimulation of a city and the friendliness of a neighborhood, have privacy and potluck dinners, freedom and responsibility, where all the adults take responsibility to help all the children; make connection without becoming clannish, and provide accountability without autocratic control. The ideal community supports individual growth and development, and fosters loyalty and commitment to the common good.

That's us, or rather, the Unitarian Universalist Congregation of Fort Wayne!

—Ruth Imler Langhinrichs

Ruth and Dick celebrate Easter with daisies at the
UU Congregation in Fort Wayne, Indiana

Reflections of Minister's Wife

At the time of this writing; I am a minister's wife of fifteen years' experience, including three as a *divinity dame* at the Harvard Divinity School, a wife of twenty years, the mother of sixteen- and eighteen-year old daughters, and a member of the working force (part-time or full-time for thirty-nine years), including time spent working first toward a master's degree in social work and then the completion of a master's degree in English.

Such self-revelatory facts—and subsequent others—are only significant because they can serve as a frame of reference for the questions I am about to raise in response to a request to do so from the ad hoc leadership of an informal gathering of minister's mates (MM) at the UU General Assembly in Ithaca, New York, in June [1977]. Since I am a *wife*, I am speaking to other wives, but would welcome amplification or supplementation from female ministers and their mates or those individuals among us who are concerned with purpose and goals of a revitalized organization of UU Minister's Mates and its relation to the Unitarian Universalist Minister's Association (UUMA), the theological schools and the UUA itself.

To use Gail Sheehy's label from her book *Passages*, I am a *delayed nurturer*. I had a career before marriage and then happily chose to become a wife and mother at the age of 35. To invent a label, the man I married is a *delayed minister*, inasmuch as he considered the ministry after graduation from high school, but did not act upon his urge until the age of 41, when his successful business career proved to be boringly stultifying and morally unacceptable on occasion. His spiritual background, like my own, consisted of faithful Sunday School attendance (his in a Presbyterian church and mine in a Baptist), religious disenchantment in college, devastating disillusionment during WWII, subsequent intellectual flirtation with Marxism and Freudism, and then a return to religion in the '50s, he to

First UU Church, Detroit and me to First Church, Philadelphia, where Harry Schofield was then minister.

Thus, as individuals we: (1) are not born UUs and may still be grappling with subconscious ministerial role expectations of the more traditional Protestantism of the 1920s and '30s; (2) have experienced the conflict between personal, materialistic success and social service commitments; and (3) have developed highly individualistic, independent lifestyles before marriage.

As a couple, we have *gone to Harvard Divinity School together*, questioned our relationship to our congregation and to each other. Is it a contract or a commitment? Is his work a profession or a calling? And we struggle continuously with responsibilities and implications of our answers and choices—including whether to participate in UU General Assemblies, one or both of us, most years since 1961.

In the belief that confession strengthens the soul and with the hope it may spark other Ministers' Mates (MM) to risk sharing some of their experiences, successful or other, I spill out these observations.

The twin demons recreation and money, for instance, frequently lead me to a third resentment. Most of my best friends and playmates are members of the congregation and I know they love us; yet sometimes I feel I am too dependent on their financial goodwill. I am uncomfortably defensive if I possess and enjoy a dress with a designer's label (*it was on sale*) or serve strawberries out of season (*they were left over on Sunday at the super mart*). I matter, too. "Why can't we party on Saturday night with our friends just once in a while?" (I work Monday through Friday.) "Why do we have to be in church when everybody else seemingly takes advantage of the long week-ends with Monday holidays?" I brood, too. "Why does my husband check out the RE Department or listen to the guest speaker when I think he should take a Sunday off?"

Superficial problems, I suppose—except that for me, at this time in my life, they are more like symptoms of a debilitating ailment I've come to call the dead-center syndrome. Although I'm the first to admit that I haven't been the most sacrificial wife in the UU ministry, I do have a nagging hang-over of an inner, society-implanted question: *have we gotten ahead?* Occasionally, and privately, I speculate as to what that could mean; the wife of the UUA president or the UU church with largest membership, or one with the largest budget or with the most distinguished membership, or of the most prestigious design, or on the east or west coast? Or should I be content to live wherever we land as if indeed it is heaven on earth? And if I do not, what is the matter with me, my values?

Why, for instance, is money nudging its way up on my list of priorities, in a way and into a position I never imagined it would? Maybe its inflation—that college education for our daughters is something they'll have to acquire by grant personhood and that retirement or even semi-retirement looks bleak. Or is it just me?

Am I a problem? I'd like to think that it depends on who you ask. I have come a long way: I'm now less likely to blame him or them and more likely to look at (not blame for the most part) myself. I was the eldest child in my family—and that usually means bossiness and ambitiousness, as well as an inclination to nurture. And I *am* doing something about my unmet needs: working, sharing where I am and risking. I'm even assuming here the responsibility for having married the man and supporting his decision to become a minister!

Yet I do continue to struggle with my feelings. I do feel wiped out when my husband and I, as a couple, meet new people and I am ignored; I do feel the need of a more affirmative, zestful, loving attitude toward the institution of the church and toward all the members of the congregation, not *just* the congenial others like myself; I do feel guilty about the minor, I hope, gossip I exchange and that our home life is not only just like that of everybody else, but probably only a little worse in terms of mundane bickering over the use of the car, spending money and allocation of chores.

From such personal risk-taking, I cautiously continue—not leap—to propose that we exchange in greater depth and perhaps with more honesty our experiences and expectations for ourselves as MMs in the UUA.

At the next General Assembly, for instance, I'd like to explore further the issues or folk beliefs or realities that emerged from our meeting in Ithaca, New York that: (1) our husbands are professionals not unlike doctors or teachers; (2) that people from the church are our greatest source of recreation and support; (3) that a UU congregation, different from the traditionalists, doesn't expect a mate to be anyone other than himself or herself; (4) that the time a MM family spends together during the summer compensates for the weekends we miss ten months a year and all the hurried or interrupted dinner hours.

I don't want gripe sessions, but rather growing—or, if that cliché word is offensive—*gaining* sessions. I'd just like to know more about making the most of being a minister's wife and about a minister's marriage.

I'd like our group (the MM) to design a questionnaire concerning our educational backgrounds, professions, employment, number and ages of children. I'd like to listen to a panel discussion of how different MMs *put it together*; I'd like other delegates to see us as we see ourselves; I'd like some fun time together and with our mates.

I'd like the planning committee to provide child care, meeting room space and program support. I'd like a program, a workshop for those married MMs present to open and/or re-open the delicate question of clarifying and testing our mutual expectations and role images. Have they become anachronistic and/or personally impossible? If so, what can we do about it?

We need casebook materials presenting the sorts of situations both younger and older MMs face. We need role models and discussion leaders and small group discussions where we can develop the confidentiality to consider such sticky matters as personal goals, feelings about incomes not proportionate to the training and deprivation undergone earlier, the feelings of mates and congregation as we seek additional employment for personal satisfaction and to supplement family income—and the potential backlash of inadequate salary increases for our mates if we earn substantial amounts of money or achieve worldly success, the nature of family spiritual life, if any, our jealousy of the church as a rival for our mate's affection, the burned-out, over-committed husband (yes, even our sex lives), the cynicism or bitterness we may experience when our basic dedication and good intentions are eroded by feelings of deprivation.

And I'd like the UUMA and our own congregations and our mates to acknowledge our personhood by listening to our needs, supporting our programs and acting on our recommendations. Mates need sabbaticals too. Mates need to be included in retirement planning seminars. Or are we? Mates need to know more about themselves and why they have chosen to marry a service-motivated individual and why that person, in turn, chose his/her mate and the ministry. We need to know the facts about such practical matters as budget-planning, insurance, pension funds and college opportunities for our children. If and when our mates *move on or ahead* we need to know what a new congregation expects in a minister's mate (if they really know) and if they will help us, as females, to find new positions also.

Finally, if I do understand not only what I feel, but what I think, I'm issuing a call for the organization of a continental network of individuals whose concern extend beyond a haphazard reunion at a General Assembly, happy and useful as those occasions may sometimes be. Through district meetings, theological schools, study groups and/or outside experts, now is the time for an investigation of such primary issues as: (1) the actual adherence of ministers and congregations to the UUMA guidelines; 2b) the hidden expectations of our most enlightened congregations; (3) the impact of any pre-UU religious connection on our self-expectations and (4) the psychological strengths of those ministers and MMs who choose to stay married and in the ministry.

—Ruth Imler Langhinrichs [1977]

Response:

Like Ruth, I am a minister's wife. To some, it may seem that our similarities end there. We are from different generations, parts of the country and spiritual backgrounds; and I am still new in my role as wife of the minister, even though Misty-Dawn and I have been married for over 13 years, she is currently serving her third year of her first settled ministry. Yet some of our experiences are very much the same. Neither of us knew when we said, "I do," that we would eventually become a *minister's wife*.

While many of the questions, concerns and suggestions Ruth raises are also relevant for me, I think some progress has been made toward connecting and supporting UU ministers' partners and spouses (UUMPs) over the years. Also the UUA and UUMA are trying to prepare prospective ministers and their families for the challenges that will lie ahead. For example, ministers are reminded of the importance of self-care throughout the fellowship process and congregations are asked to describe the expectations they may have of their new minister's family during the search process.

I don't know if MM is a predecessor to UUMPs, but UUMPs is the current group that sounds closest to Ruth's descriptions of MM. We have connection through an email listserv, and have recently added a closed Facebook group—both online groups are only for the partners and spouses of ministers (including retired ministers and seminarians), and expect confidentiality of the information shared amongst the group. Unfortunately, my work schedule prevents me from attending many denominational events, such as General Assembly and district or regional gatherings, so I find the online connections to be vital. However, I yearn for some of the deeply supportive network Ruth has sought, as described in her final call and hopes for developing *gaining* sessions.

It is a challenging and rewarding life we lead!

—Jenna Gervasi-Shelly, 2015

Unitarian Universalist Meetinghouse in Fort Wayne 1965

Reflections of Minister's Daughter

Dear Bobbi:

Sorry for the delay responding to your request for family info about my father. Do not take this to mean that I am unexcited about the upcoming book. Rather it reflects my inability to adequately describe my father in words; he was a really interesting and complex man—and the fact that I am unsure. I do hope that you have a copy of the funeral service—I said many of the important things there.

Regardless, in some ways my father's life assumes almost mythic proportions. He was a war hero, a Marine, one of the few officers of his battalion to survive the Battle of Saipan. And, at the other extreme, a minister and a pacifist who actively protested our involvement in Vietnam. I had trouble synthesizing all the opposites and contradictions he presented.

One of the things that most impressed me was my father's amazing memory—especially for historical events. As a child I rarely bothered to use an encyclopedia. It was always easier to ask my dad. Likewise, even when he was sick and in the hospital, it frequently seemed as if he knew the names of the orderlies taking care of him—their names, where they went to school, etc. He was quite beloved for this ability.

My father was also deeply connected to the Midwest. I used to love driving to Iowa with him to visit relatives because I imagined how much he loved the country we passed through: the openness of it, the green, the fields and the long view of sky. He grew up on the banks of the Mississippi and would tell stories of his canoe trips with boyhood friends. I believe friends from his high school are still close and see each other regularly.

My father was not especially materialistic, but he had fine tastes. He liked things of quality—food of quality, ideas of quality and people of quality Although he deeply loved living in Fort Wayne, he never gave up his New York Saks Fifth Avenue charge card or his Boston Harvard Coop charge card. Somehow, I have inherited both of these now.

I don't know what place there is in your book for my father's more difficult and more painful habits and experiences. He was not a particularly happy man most of the time I knew him. I think he was lonely often at the Meetinghouse—maybe at some level fundamentally lonely. I remember he once told me that *the loving yourself stuff* was a bunch of crap.

I frequently wished that my father would learn to love himself more. Anyway, I would be willing to share more thoughts and recollections with you (about how he shared religion with me as a child or other topics).

Overall, as I grew up, I wanted more of a relationship with my father. I did many things to please him (drama, extemporaneous speaking and cheerleading, to name a few). His approval has always meant a good deal to me—for good or for ill.

I have been very busy planning for our wedding and responding to your letter has felt overwhelming to me. I feel like I am walking a bit of a tightrope, wanting to provide the most positive picture of my father that I can honestly provide and fearing that truthful answers to your questions might anger and disappoint you and others.

I don't remember any Bible stories or morality/ethical lessons. In fact, I remember my parents not sharing their opinions because they were afraid they might unduly influence me developing my own.

I was in an unusual situation because I went to kindergarten at Redeemer Lutheran, because I missed the public school age cut-off by 30 days but was ready to start school. There I learned to pray and I remember feeling that I was more Christian/religious than my family. This was true again in high school when I belonged to Campus Life and wanted to be baptized by a friend who was a Christian minister. My father never verbalized any disapproval, but my mother told me later that these choices of mine bothered him a great deal.

As a kid, I don't remember anything about the *Great Beyond*. I wasn't even sure if my dad believed in God. I think he got more spiritual as he aged and confronted death and his own mortality.

My mom was more influential on my reading than my dad was, and still is. I think my mom was a force behind my dad's reading, too. I do remember my dad as having an amazing memory for historical information and loving fine things, but my mom supplied us all with books.

I think I have more memories of my dad as a dad—the fact that he was a minister only affected my life in tangential ways—like the fact that he often worked nights and weekends and that Sundays tended to be stressful. I frequently wished my dad would hurry up after church, instead of talking so much so we could go home and have lunch!

I was very proud of my dad for his participation in the Paris peace talks. I remember being very excited because the church got broken into (perhaps by the FBI). This made my dad seem very glamorous to me.

My dad has had a large impact on my career choices, however. He really wanted me to pursue acting, but…as a kid, a friend and I used to perform funeral services for dead animals (slugs, squirrels, etc.) I used to write the eulogy. Also, whenever kids in the church had problems like ones I had (wear an eye patch for a lazy eye), my dad would have them come talk to me, very similar to being a psychologist now!

—Jenny Langhinrichs, 1992

Dick on Father's Day 1968 with the family dog,
Haile Selassie, a gift from a Peace Corp Volunteer

Impact on the Wider Community

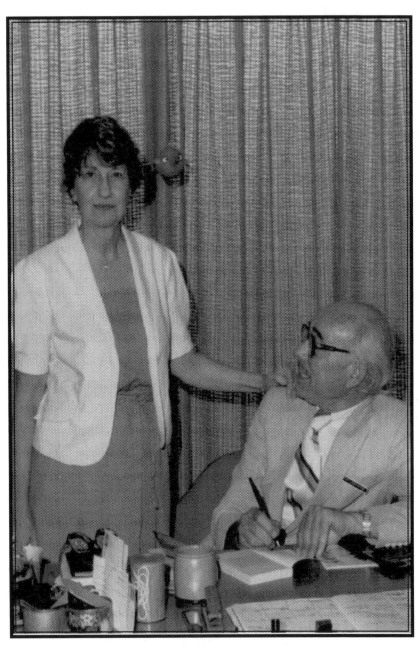

Ruth and Dick at his desk discussing
the possibility of a date night

The Function of UU Ministry

Each Unitarian Universalist congregation is a self-selecting community of persons who perceive that the most basic characteristic of all known life is change. The members of our churches—some consciously, but many without clear recognition—are involved in uncovering and sustaining an awareness of the sacred within this matrix of change. In contrast, religious orthodoxy in all traditions pursues the delusion of permanence, of changelessness, and defines the sacred in terms of fixed, unalterable categories of perfection.

The function of the Unitarian Universalist minister, then, is joyously to affirm change as a basic characteristic of life and to elucidate the sacred within that context. This he seeks to do through the richness of his own lifestyle, his choices and decisions, his friendships, his actions in the public realm and, especially, through his performance of the traditional ministerial functions: leading in worship, preaching, counseling, education and the celebration of rites of passage such as birth, maturity, marriage and death. He seeks serenely to attune himself to, and to place his faith in, the power of love: affirming love's potential to deepen all human experience, to sustain hope, to create beauty, to reveal truth—in every human life and life experience.

—**Rev. Richard Langhinrichs**

A Dearth of Theology

[**Editor's Note:** The Fortnightly Club, organized in 1892, was the first club in Fort Wayne for the purpose of discussing intellectual and cultural matters by both men and women. Dick Langhinrichs served a term as president. The following is from a speech he gave to the club:]

Over the last few months I have been gathering together those things that I thought would be most significant to share with you this evening. I discovered that indeed there is no dearth of theology. Nevertheless, as you may have figured out for yourselves, I was making a play on the word dearth and its connection with death and the so-called *Death of God* theological movement with which the 1960s concluded. There are those who indeed claim that theology, the Queen of the Sciences, is all but dead in our day. Emotionally and experientially, I can understand why this opinion, this perception may be widespread among us.

As some of you know, I made the decision to enter the ministry in midlife at age forty-one. Ruth, our two daughters, who were then infants—one was six months old and the other was two years and seven months old—and I moved from Detroit to Cambridge, Massachusetts; and I enrolled in June of 1962 at the Harvard Divinity School. The first summer my assignment was to learn (in six weeks) to read Koine Greek. Learning to read Greek in six weeks at any age, I suspect, would be difficult. At age forty-one, and having been out of college for twenty years, it was quite an obstacle course!

I allude to this because at that time, in that summer as we passed through Harvard Square, there were bookstores abounding all about the square; and everywhere on the public walks and sidewalks, there were copies of the works of Paul Tillich, of the existential theologians. Paul Tillich was on the faculty of Harvard, at the Episcopal Theological School, with Dr. Joseph Fletcher, who was just then about to become especially notorious and, in some quarters, thoroughly disliked for his work on the new morality. He was teaching young Richard Niebuhr, who was on the faculty at Harvard, while Reyhold, his uncle, and Richard, his father, were both still alive and producing theology: Vatican II was convened, people from the Harvard faculty were among those distinguished guests from the United States who were invited to participate in Rome.

In 1963–64, Cardinal Butrick, one of the key figures at Vatican II, was invited to the United States and conducted a symposium. There were so many requests for tickets that they had to hold it in a very ancient building on the Harvard campus that had been constructed in the 19th century—a kind of an open coliseum area where everyone who wanted to attend and see or hear Cardinal Butrick could indeed attend.

Then came Montgomery and Selma, and as from Fort Wayne and other parts of the country, tens and hundreds of religious people immigrated—took planes, buses, trains, drove—to Alabama to witness race relations. My vivid recollection of that is that as some of those persons returned, they used a theological term that they had experienced—kiros, the presence of the Holy Spirit, the togetherness of the church. They said that it was a great moment in American religion, and a personal experience of great significance.

In contrast to that, I think we would all have to agree that the 1970s have been a pretty colorless era and a rather negative, discouraging one, especially as far as public interest in theology is concerned. There would be, I think, no American clergy *person* (as we have learned to say), either male or female, of the serious distinguished stature of persons like Butrick.

In addition to that, I think that there has been, as all the polls indicate, a significant decline in attendance and in participation in our religious life in the United States. So in addressing this problem, it has been a perplexity to me as to whether I ought really to talk about the status of the church in our time or the status of theology. These things clearly are interrelated whether or not you think of theology as being a very significant part of what goes on in church on Sundays or at other times.

To further under gird and emphasize the current vast number of theologies, I selected out of a number of possible others, this statement by Seth Hall from the March 17, 1976 issue of *Christian Century*. That was the year of America's Bicentennial, if you recall, and there was a burst of retrospective and current assessments of what was going on in the field of religion. Already people were regretting the passage of this great era of theology that seemed to conclude with the death of Tillich and Carl Hearth, the great Swiss neo-orthodox theologian.

Seth Hall, however, claimed there was indeed no dearth:

> There are theologies of biography, black liberation, change, culture, death of God, ecumenics, fantasy, freedom, history, holocaust, hope, humor, imagination, joy, liberation, love, mystery, myth, narrative, paradox, peace, personality, play, politics, process, psychotherapy, revolution, story, symbol, tradition, transcendence, transubstantiation and woman's liberation—each representing a distinct point of view and each laying claim to priority on the agenda of the entire theological community.

The possibilities in that quotation are not yet exhausted. There are always candidates waiting in the wings to be signed up for a tour on the electra circuit or a temporary run on the best seller charts; so new special kinds of theologies continue to proliferate up to this very moment.

As another illustration that there is indeed no dearth of theology is the result of a survey conducted by Dean K. Thompson, published in 1977, which explored how many people were pursuing theology in the United States. He sent questionnaires to every seminary, university, theological school, and all universities that had departments of religion. He got, in a blind mailing, 899 replies from individuals who identified themselves as being theologians here in the United States in 1977, and this was their first professional priority. That they were involved in pursuing theology indicates that not only do we not have a dearth of theology but we also do not have a dearth of people who are seriously undertaking the pursuit of theology.

In addition to that, I want to point to a few books that during the 1970s, while not theological, have very profoundly addressed themselves to the situation in which our society finds itself and from them, have generated viewpoints that have been very provocative to the theological community or that reflect some of the problems that are perceived by persons who describe themselves as being full time theologians. One that is most popular and has been, perhaps, most widely criticized by some (and has been on the best seller list for about eighteen months) is Christopher Lash's *The Culture of Evil* and also *The Denial of Death*, a Pulitzer Prize winner—all these are very serious books by non-theologians. A third and a fourth that I know many persons both from my own religious tradition and many others have read and discussed and have found provocative, sometimes devastating, but significant: Richard Sennet's *The Fall of Public Man*, and Ann Douglas' *The Feminization of American Culture*. There are others that you might also want to add to this list.

But what we experienced at the end of the 1960s and early 70s was the excitement over the *death of God* and theology; and the new morality *situation ethics* began to wane. With the increase in concern over our involvement in the Vietnam War, perhaps related or perhaps with no connection at all—came an interest for religiosity and especially, interest in religions other than Christianity.

For a brief period of time, many people, especially young people, took off and became seriously interested in Hinduism, Buddhism, Sufism, a form of Islam, and so forth. This, undoubtedly, was attributed to such groups as the Beatles, who after they decided that drugs were not the total solution for their spiritual difficulties, hooked up with an Indian teacher and flew off to India. As soon as they did that, hundreds of others followed and the rash of immigration to India during the late 60s and early 70s was widespread. The effect that it had here in the United States, however, was that most of our major universities, which previously had not had a department of religion, established one. Also, there was very heavy enrollment in philosophy courses and courses in religion in 1971 through 1973, which has declined every year since. Indiana University established a Department of Religion in Bloomington with a very distinguished man at its head, whom I shall quote later, William May. Today, however, the number of students enrolled in that department or studying religion as a major is slim compared to what it was in the early 1970s. One young man who went through that period about a year ago is a member of our church. He brought me all of these books and said that he didn't have a need for them anymore and he wanted to know if I could use them or give them away to somebody else who would like to have them—all of his textbooks.

As May described it to me in a conversation I had about this, he said it was like a romance. Someone falling in love with a person whom one only knows from a distance can, therefore, be idealized; and as people became more fully familiar in a totality with other religions, they found in them as many flaws and defects as the various forms of Christianity to which we ascribe and which we are critical of in our society, but to which an abundance of people are committed to this religion, flaws or not.

So having said all this then, who are the theologians? What are the theological issues that are being studied, that are being written about? Are they matters of concern to us? First of all, despite what I have said about the establishment of programs and religion and departments of religion, there continues to be a widespread interest in a variety of ways to mythical spirituality and a response to this on the part of theologians—a concerned response, a critical response. The sociological components of this mystical spirituality are, for one thing, an experience and a program which you may have encountered directly.

Some persons whom I know of in our denomination have been involved in a program with respect to *the extended family.* The idea of this was to gather into greater intimacy that part of the development of a significant spiritual life in close intimate relationships with other human beings— something that was denied in our impersonal society. This was connected with mysticism and spirituality in the sense that out of this reaffirmation of intense significant inter-personal relationships, there would automatically develop some deeper conception of the relationship to the wholeness of all being. The component of this was something that I would term *intensified intimacy.*

We gradually, though sometimes not so gradually, radically moved in the 1960s and 70s in to what was termed at the time *letting it all hang out.* You can still hear that term occasionally—with its total candor, rejection of any right to privacy about one's personal life, and the premise that the more everybody knew about each other, the better. Theology has responded, as well as the popular non-theological press, with some concerns.

First of all, as the serious scholars have moved into the study of myth and legend and the significance of some of our early traditions such as the

Adonic myth, or the story from Genesis (whether or not in your religious view it is myth or history) and the implications of the story of Adam and the significance of shame, and the desire for privacy. This concern has been explored in a variety of cultures by different people. For example, a book, by Carl Schneider, a very widely read theological book, *Shame, Exposure, and Privacy*, is a rejection of the notion that the most significant way in which we can develop ourselves spiritually or psychologically is through relinquishment of privacy or the total abandonment of privacy.

At another level we encounter Christopher Lasch and his critique of *The Culture of Narcissism*. The effect of religion in the 1970s took this particular form. Much of Judaism and Christianity proved a means through which these concepts were introduced. The focus of this line of thinking was to neglect the public realm and to emphasize the individual person above all else.

Thus, my feeling good is more important than anything else in the world; my having significant interpersonal-relationships is more important than anything else that may happen in the world. What goes on in public is something that I have to, perhaps, put up with to a limited degree; but the less time that I have to spend at my job or being involved in politics or community affairs, the better off I am. Now, one can, of course, trace this idea and the effect it has had on theology and the church back as early as the 1950's, and to the gradual decline in the relationship of human beings in our Western culture to public life, including how we in the church relate to it, back to the 17th century. Be that as it may, I think you all can relate as I do, as I am able to, to the popular magazine prescription of the 1950s which in effect was saying "You're never going to get any happiness out of your job."

Remember that was the era when there was great criticism of conformity; we were all conformists. People today say that college kids are moving back into the 1950s—as if it had been a time when no one was critical of what was going on in the world. Yet, there *was* a great deal of criticism about bureaucratic conformity, conformity to the industrial hierarchy, the firm for which one worked, how much one's job depleted one and that the only solution was to develop a happy family life—get married, have several kids, get yourself a barbecue pit (in those days, not many of us had enough money to build our own swimming pool). But the idea was:

we did what we had to do in the public realm in order to make a living and in order to really find happiness from the public realm.

By the 1970s both non-religious and religious figures are calling this *narcissism*. Every individual is looking, seeking to find his or her personal happiness at the neglect of any loyalty or commitment to a group of any sort. It has gradually become apparent, and this is a matter of deep concern to theologians, that Christianity (and I would include Judaism, for our Jewish friends, both in this group and in the community who are experiencing similar problems in Western culture.) This does not mean that people don't go to church or that they don't maintain some kind of connection to one. Indeed, here in the United States, it is estimated that about 60% of the people still belong to a religious organization and on a typical weekend about 40% attend church.

As you know, too, if you travel to Western Europe, you can go to some of the great cathedrals in England and if you bother to attend or to hear magnificent music, there will be a choir of twenty men and boys and five priests and you may be the only attendee there. That is far more characteristic not only of England but of Sweden, Germany and, to a lesser degree, our whole Western civilization. Religion and especially Christianity in many of its respects has become marginal. Therefore, theologians are addressing themselves to the question of why this is so. The ways in which we are responding, I think, are equally significant.

First of all, one way in which various religious figures have found to respond to this question, is to find ways in the *if you can't lick 'em, join 'em* train of thought to hook up with the multimedia people. We see a good deal of this going on here in the United States, where some religious figures are using the media to develop a huge national following. Although true for all theologians, this attitude is best represented by Eugon Multman, a German theologian and a reformed minister, who fortunately, was here at First Presbyterian Church under their sponsorship. He emphasizes the necessity of re–establishing a community—to accept the beginning premise that for most persons today, that the church has become irrelevant, that religion has become irrelevant because it is not speaking meaningfully and forcefully to people, or it is doing so in a way that is down-right boring.

The solution to this is to counteract this multimedia Christianity by working to establish significant interpersonal relationships that do not emphasize intimacy so much as they do diversity and group commitment to certain goals or principals in the larger community.

There are difficulties with this solution, however, which a number of people (and this is where Professor May from Bloomington is very helpful, I think) are up against with religion and Christianity. One of the difficulties is that the bureaucratization of American life and the response of most religious institutions, either individually or denominationally, have been to bureaucratize themselves and to be swallowed up in our cultures rather unconsciously by doing so. The effective bureaucracy, as you know, whether it is political or religious, exists to give very ordinary people the power to do things that may be extraordinary—or may be downright dreadful.

At any event, most of us as human beings (and this is where the establishment of community and figures like Hans Kung to whom I will refer to in another context, the German who has had some difficulty with the Catholic Church) feel that the church must put itself into a tension with the whole thrust toward the establishment of bureaucracy on a national and multinational level in our time.

An illustration that May used in his presentation that was very striking to me was a reference to the National Council of Churches in the American Baptist Church which has repeatedly taken positions that were somewhat critical of the activities of the Dow Chemical Company. All of this activity was done on a national level and some of it in coordination with other church persons at the top bureaucracy. There were decisions that were entered into by some other people but ultimately made by people who were in charge of the bureaucratic proceedings of the American Baptist Church. It was only after they had been somewhat frustrated and had very little effect with whatever they wished to accomplish with Dow Chemical Company (as my understanding of the story as it was told to me two or three years ago) that someone discovered that there is a very active viable Baptist church in Midland, Michigan and most of the top executives in the Dow Chemical Company attend that church. Nobody had ever gone to talk to them about the inter-connection with whatever they were doing and how they were functioning as Baptists. It was an encounter between bureaucracy and bureaucracy, and not one of personal contacts. Whether or not that is a good example in terms of interest or legitimate concerns of the church, it illustrates well, I think, the concerns that many theological people have.

My reflection on this leads me to pose to you a question, which principal excellent theologians, and Multman, who is certainly one of the foremost theologians, direct us to the establishments of communities: is this merely nostalgia from the past—a nostalgia for the Biblical model of the small community that we really could understand? Or is this a genuine, challenging alternative to the bureaucracy in our time?

The dynamics, whether it is in Multman's thinking or elsewhere in any of the other writers of how the small community of believers in one church in Fort Wayne, Indiana, can radically and adequately respond to what happens to us as a result of the bureaucratization of life in the world is beyond my power to perceive. I understand the intention, and I too feel good about the small groups in small communities, but I think it leaves some of the issues unresolved.

So, also, I think of the church in a very divided position along with the theologians and thinkers in terms of how to relate to the media. I've already alluded to this but there is a larger problem, and it can be sub-divided into three key theological issues, in addition to the sociological ones.

The Question of Authority

The first is *authority*. This is where Hans Kung has gotten himself into difficulty with the Catholic Church in Germany. It is the subject, however, of most of the work of every theologian, and it has a great deal to do with the question of the media in this respect. Theology is concerned with stating the positions of a Christian Church or a Christian thinker or Christianity as a whole, on an issue or on a series of issues. Whether or not you read that person, whether or not his views or her views are taken seriously, depends upon their authority. It depends on who is speaking, who believes that when that person speaks, the words ought to be heeded. Now this is a question clearly as old as religion. You can go back into the earliest accounts in the Old Testament.

This is an aside: I came here this evening direct from teaching a philosophy class at IU-PU. The reading for class tonight was from John

Paul Sartre, who used the illustration of Abraham going up on Mount Myriq to sacrifice Isaac as a basis for his on a question in his great essay, *What is Existentialism?* (published in 1945). How did Abraham know that that was, as he puts it, an angel speaking to him? Sartre was wrong to question it; a good Bible course is needed here. It was God speaking to Abraham. But even more so, how would he know it was God? That is the ultimate religious question of authority, obviously. When someone tells you, "This is God speaking. These are God's words," how do you know to believe that person?

We are encountering it now in the media. How much credibility do you give to Oral Roberts or to any of the other people who are spending millions of dollars for religion on the media? If you want to tell people that we should not give credibility to them, on what grounds do you say, "This person is not a legitimate preacher or prophet or teacher or thinker and someone else is?" What are the ways in which we discriminate those persons who are to be believed and heeded from those who are not to be believed and heeded?

This is a problem much larger than the theological issue in our society and permeates all of our public life. This is why I recommend to you a book like Paul Sennet's *The Fall of Public Man,* which raises a question as to the credibility of any elected official or any attorney or physician. Credibility in every professional area has deteriorated in our time. The church particularly is faced with this problem.

This is why Hans Kung, whose two key issues, theologically, are the authority of the Pope and the divinity of Jesus, experienced difficulty with the Catholic Church. So that you clearly understand, those of you who are non-Catholic and those of you that are Catholics who are not familiar with this, what the church ultimately decided to do after trying to get the Vatican to deal with Kung's questioning, was to arrange for the University of Tubingen to no longer retain him as their official Catholic teacher. And yet, neither did it try to ban any of his works nor did it excommunicate him. As well as I know, the church is not even planning to try him for heresy. It was a matter of authority.

And these are the kinds of issues that have plagued almost every religious denomination—Christian and Jewish, in the last ten years. It was a matter of who has the right to speak for the Catholic Church; and the people in Rome said that given the particular things Hans Kung wants to teach right now, he should not be our official spokesman at the University of Tubingen. As I understand it, Tubingen is going to go right on allowing him to teach (which I think will please some people both in the Catholic community as well as in the Protestant community—it remains a matter of a church funded religion, however). This authority—authenticity question then very directly relates to all of our lives today.

The Question of Evil and Sin

The second issue after authority is the question of *evil and sin*. Or, if you want this two issues, evil and sin, and death. Within the church generally (and then very much in part of media Christianity as we are encountering it), but especially in the last 100 years, there has been the matter of emphasizing the goodness of God and de-emphasizing the evil that we, human beings have done, are doing, are capable of doing and the consequences of this and the relationship that this has to any kind of significant religious belief.

The most severe criticisms of the so-called liberal churches or of the social gospel in the late 19th and early 20th Century (that some would say culminated in 1964) was that Protestants and Catholics were urged to be very judgmental about the sins of others while being very self-forgiving about their own shortcomings.

So, the theological book, if you were going to read any theological work that has been produced in recent years, is not written by a theologian but a French Catholic philosopher that everyone, from the most conservative side of the religious spectrum to the most liberal, has read and praised as being one of the finest pieces of theological thinking and writing that has been produced in a long time is Paul Renoir's *The Symbolism of Evil.*

This book also gets into continuing issues which perplex theologians, like the tension or conflict between science and religion, between history and religion, whether or not some of the parts of the sacred writings are mythological or historical, if they are anti-scientific, are they fully reconcilable with scientific viewpoints, and the simple question of do they have significance? The remarkable thing about Renoir's work is that while he, for example, takes the position of the creation stories in the Bible as mythological, persons who don't think that they are can still read it and see that they are useful and reconcile some of the tension between science and religion. I began this paper with a presentation of all kinds of theology that are being given today. I did this with a purpose because it makes my head swim, and I am professionally committed to theology. The effect that this has on you, or must have on people in general, is confusion and questioning of the totality of the authority of any particular religious position (as many illustrations have been given also where people's response is ho-hum).

The Question of the Kingdom of God

The third theological issue is the Kingdom of God (or whatever language you might want this in, this being the most typical theological language). And that is....perhaps for another time!

Minister-on-Exchange to London

[**Editor's Note:** Arrangements were made through the Minister-on-Exchange program for Dick and his family to exchange pulpits and activities with a minister and family from London, starting August 1, 1973 through December 31, 1973. Below is a letter that Ruth and Dick sent to friends back in the U.S. toward the end of their stay in London.]

Dear Betty and Jim,

Like that more widely known traveler we, too, have left some things undone, which we ought to have done, and done, alas, some things which we ought not to have done—and here it is nearly six month's distance from Fort Wayne, Indiana, USA and the Unitarian Congregation there.

Nevertheless, we have made a valiant attempt to absorb all the delightful opportunities our gracious host, All Soul's Unitarian Church of Golder's Green, planned for us. Our daughters, for example, are attending the *posh* Channing School for Girls which was originally founded for the daughters of Unitarian ministers; I teach one day a week there. Dick is teaching two days a week at Christ's College for Boys. (As you may remember, the exchange between the two congregations included the pulpits and any other regularly scheduled activities. I will be eager to learn how Keith and Judy Gilley and their son fared in our Fort Wayne lives and activities!)

Even as we are slowly becoming addicted to tea, high, low or anytime, however, we, as you so astutely put it, Jim, are ever aware that we are indeed representing the United States. And that has not always been an easy or pleasant mission. After the perfunctory hospitality and discreet informational exchanges, we eventually discovered the awful truth: most Americans are considered to be materialistic, exploitive, shallow and gullible. How else to explain Watergate? You can imagine, Betty, how puffed up I was to learn from my students that our daughters were not *dim* like most Americans.

Your thoughtful farewell note—with its unmistakable support—was a great source of encouragement. And we thank you for it. We are looking forward to telling you our tales soon after our return next month—and happily over the dinner table.

—Affectionately, Ruth and Dick

Church Family Ties

[**Editor's Note:** The following letters were written to a friend of Dick's, who lived in San Diego]

Dear Helen,

I was excited—and very touched—to hear from you—Sad for me to think of Carl as gone. Jack Bowen had written about this. Glad to hear that Toni is with you and that you have such a beautiful home.

San Diego seems to be a second or alternative home for many Fort Wayne Unitarians; four church families have connections there. On Christmas Eve I had the pleasure and honor of christening a baby boy who was born in San Diego last June, the son of a couple I married in 1976 (the father grew up in this church and was very active in our youth group) and the grandson of devoted members here who are also close personal friends. Two other members are in San Diego at the moment visiting children.

—Love and peace, Richard and Ruth, December 28, 1978

Dear Helen,

We have snow on the ground and it was ten below zero this morning when I drove our seventeen- year-old daughter to high school before sun-up; I would be delighted to be in Escondido this afternoon.

Our holidays are hectic because of my profession. This year, it was particularly so, as our older daughter, Julie, a nineteen-year-old sophomore at Swarthmore, a Quaker college near Philadelphia, brought a male classmate along for the festivities. He was our house-guest for two weeks and proved to be a very likable young man who added much to the festivities—and to the usual confusion! Thus, this letter was begun and then set aside. Brian, the young man, has returned to Pennsylvania; and Julie departs on the evening train—if it arrives (it's usually hours behind schedule!)

This is our fourteenth year in Fort Wayne. We have two daughters, both of whom were born at Harper Hospital, Detroit, before I left the laundry and went to Harvard to study for the ministry. Julie is a dancer and writer-editor, reading for honors in religion at college. Jennifer, a junior in high school, is a scholar and an actress/cheerleader. Ruth taught for Purdue for several years and now is Writer-in-Residence for the Fine Arts Foundation, where she edits a quarterly newspaper and does a multitude of other creative things as well. In 1973 we lived in London, England for six months; I ministered to a Unitarian congregation there while their English minister and family came here to Fort Wayne and served this church. We have traveled extensively over the years—tent camping all over the U.S.A, Canada, and even into Mexico in 1970—and to Europe and North Africa (Morocco) as well. In February, Ruth and I have been invited to participate in a seminar for Christian leaders in Israel. We are booked to spend two weeks there and hope to make a stop in Athens on our return flight (Ruth has been to Athens and Jerusalem, but I have not). We are getting quite excited about this unexpected venture.

As you can tell, life has been good to us. We have, of course, had our sorrows and disappointments as well. My father and mother both died within a few months of each other in the fall of 1972. Dad was eighty-four and mother, eighty-five. Ruth's mother, uncle (who had helped raise her), and her youngest sister all also died at this same general period ('72–'74). Those were difficult times for us. Both my brother and his wife have been ill and repeatedly hospitalized in recent years. Sally, my niece, married three times and has four children, three daughters and one son, Ricky, who is now a senior in high school. She has two grandchildren as well! Cindi, her third, is lots like Sally was at the same age. She has lived here with us in Fort Wayne over extended periods when things weren't going so well with her (or at home). She's twenty now—not married.

I have often thought of you over the years. Jack gave you the address of the first house we lived in here in Fort Wayne and moved out of over seven years ago. Fortunately, the neighbors and we are still in friendly communication! Thanks so much for your news and kind greetings.

—Love and peace, Richard and Ruth, January 9, 1979

Response to Misleading Editorial

Unitarian Universalist Congregation of Fort Wayne
5310 Old Mill Road
Fort Wayne, IN 46807
Phone: 260-744-1867

October 11, 1979

Ernest Williams, Editor
Fort Wayne News-Sentinel
600 W. Main
Fort Wayne, IN 46802

Dear Ernest:

I don't have the time or the resources at hand to provide you with precise facts. Nevertheless, I'm certain that the implications of your editorial of October 10ᵗʰ concerning the origins of the Metro Human Relations Commission are quite misleading.

When I came to Fort Wayne in 1965, there was already in existence a Mayor's Commission on Human Relations chaired by Pastor Edwin Nerger. Harold Zeis was mayor. In subsequent years a full-time executive director was hired. If my memory is correct, Alvin Wesley was the first: Carl Benson succeeded him after two or three years when Wesley left to take a position with the Urban League. Federal funding was not at issue in these decisions.

The name and some of the functions of the Mayor's Commission was changed first to the Fort Wayne and then to the Metropolitan Human

Relations Commission through a series of mayoral and city council decisions in the later 1960s and early 1970s. All of the efforts to bring the body we know today as the Metro Human Relations Commission into existence—were led by Fort Wayne citizens, especially those who were members of the Human Relations Council, a group of concerned, local volunteers which met regularly at the downtown YMCA, and of the Committee of 24. Federal funding, potential or actual had little or nothing to do at that time with the concerns of persons either in the Council or Committee of 24 to improve race relations and opportunities for all citizens in our community.

Since John Ankenruck, a historian, is responsible for your editorials, I am surprised at your publication of this misleading piece. What with persons like Paul Clarke, Elaine Wareham, Bill Chavis, Larry Burke, Clyde Adams, and Ian Rolland all actively involved in racial issues at the time to which I refer, getting the historical facts straight from people who are not radical leftists or *welfare staters* shouldn't be that much of a problem for him.

To sum up, Fort Wayne has a long, honorable history of concern about human relations and race relations. These concerns have received forthright expression by citizens of both political parties. Federal funding—or the lack of it—had nothing to do with these activities—or with their intensity.

I know you're managing a Republican newspaper and want Bob Armstrong to get reelected. He seems to be doing quite well. Factual misrepresentation by your staff seems more damaging than helpful to his cause at this time.

—Affectionately, Dick Langhinrichs

Honoring Fifteen Years of Service

[**Editor's Note**: In April 1995, Rev. David O. Rankin preached about ministry and *humanness* of ministers. That sermon won the UUA's Ministry Sunday Sermon Award, and was delivered at General Assembly in Spokane, Washington in June, 1995. Here are his thoughts on the personal requirements and job description for UU ministers:

> Personal Requirements: Firm but not rigid; honest but not rude; moral but not stuffy; humble but not servile; intelligent but not bookish; humorous but not frivolous; serious but not depressing; friendly but not superficial; clever but not scheming; prophetic but not critical of anyone.

> Job Description: Researches the universe; inspires the dull; comforts the afflicted; afflicts the comfortable; maintains the tradition; introduces the contemporary; reforms the society; raises the budget; arbitrates disputes; officiates at ceremonies; socializes with ease; stays awake at every meeting.

Rankin asks if it is possible for any man or woman to succeed at such a job; that "the minister is a dart board for every wish and whim."—Sep/Oct 1995 *World*, the Journal of the Unitarian Universalist Association.]

Apparently Dick had this ability—fifteen years and still counting.

The following is a press release from November 17, 1980:

Reverend Richard and Ruth Imler Langhinrichs and their daughters are to be honored for their fifteen years of service to the Unitarian Universalist Congregation and to the Fort Wayne community at a noon reception at the Unitarian Universalist Meetinghouse on Sunday, November 23rd [1980].

Langhinrichs was called to Fort Wayne in June, 1965, as the sixth minister of the Unitarian Congregation. A native of Rock Island, Illinois, he gained his higher education at Northwestern and Harvard Universities. The ministry is his second career. Until 1962, he was general manager of a large business in Detroit.

During his years in Fort Wayne, church membership has doubled. Langhinrichs has not only provided an able ministry to the Unitarian Church, he has been a creative leader in the community and the Unitarian Universalist denomination as well. In racial matters, he was chairman of the *Welcome Neighbor* housing program in the 1960s and was president of the Human Relations Council and a member of the Citizens for Peace and the Draft Information Center during the Vietnam War and was one of five Hoosier delegates to the Conference to End the War held in 1971 in Paris, France. He has served or currently serves on the boards of the South Side High School PTA, the Oakdale Neighborhood Association, Planned Parenthood of N.E. Indiana, Washington House, the Allen County Association for the Retarded, the Academy of Religion and Mental Health, the National Association for the Advancement of Colored People, the Indiana Civil Liberties Union, the World Friendship Center (Hiroshima, Japan) and the Fortnightly Club.

A scholar, Langhinrichs is a frequent lecturer and has taught many classes in philosophy at the IU-PU Regional Campus. He is the author of several published monographs as well. He also played several roles in theatrical productions at the Civic and First Presbyterian theatres.

In the Unitarian Universalist Association of churches, Langhinrichs recently completed a two-year term as president of the Ohio Valley District. In this capacity he served, in addition, as convenor for all twenty-three UU district presidents at their semi-annual convocations. Earlier, he served as the board of the continental Unitarian Universalist Ministers' Association and was official Unitarian Exchange Minister to London, England in

1973. Currently, he serves on a continental committee of six to advise the UUA on possible restructuring of district financing, trustee representation and boundaries.

Ruth Imler Langhinrichs has ministered to the congregation and served the community in many significant ways. A writer and editor by profession, Ms. Langhinrichs has used her special skills to enhance the religious education and adult programs of the church. Her journal, poetry and fiction writing workshops are popular with persons of all ages.

In 1977, her poetic script, *Mermaids in the Basement*, was produced as a dance/drama at the Unitarian Meetinghouse with funding from the Indiana Arts Commission and co-sponsored by the Women's Bureau. The production was subsequently videotaped, shown locally on cable TV and Channel 39, and then released for educational use nationwide.

Ruth is active in the Unitarian Universalist Association Women and Religion Committee which brings feminist insights to bear in traditional Christian theology and those conventional church practices based upon that theology. She is Public Information/Public Education Specialist at the Mental Health Center. For several years she was an English Instructor for Purdue University. She also served on the staff of the Fine Arts Foundation, where she created and edited the highly successful arts quarterly, *Discovery*. She also serves on the editorial advisory board of Fort Wayne's poetry quarterly, *The Windless Orchard* and was on the editorial board of the *Fort Wayne Forte*. She developed the original Women in Literature courses for the Women's Studies Program at the IU-PU Regional Campus.

Ms. Langhinrichs is a member of Women's Caucus for the Arts, the Philadelphia Art Alliance, National Association of Mental Health Officers, Designer/Craftsman Guild, Ex Libris Book Club, Women in Communication, the International Association of Business Communicators and the Fortnightly Club. She is a past-president of the South Side High School PTA, a former member of boards of the Martin Luther King Montessori School and the Civic Youtheatre. She also helped create the constitution for the Oakdale Neighborhood Association when it was founded.

She was educated at Northwestern, Pennsylvania, Wayne State and Purdue Universities and worked as an associate editor of the *Ladies Home Journal* in Philadelphia, prior to marriage in 1959.

The Langhinrichs have two daughters who have been prominent in the youth activities of the Unitarian Universalist Church on the local and regional levels. Julie, 21, is a senior at Swarthmore College, a coeducational Quaker institution near Philadelphia. She is majoring both in religion and in early childhood development. Jennifer, 19, is a freshperson at Brown University, Providence, Rhode Island. Both are alumnae of South Side High School.

Ruth practicing what she preaches: intensive journaling.

Surprise party for Dick's Tenth Anniversary at
the Fort Wayne UU Meetinghouse in 1975

Supporting the Equal Rights Amendment

[**Editor's Note:** With Dick's unspoken blessing, several women, who may prefer to be nameless, went through all the hymnals and changed sexist pronouns. We wrote in pencil I hope. I don't remember exactly. Dick unconditionally supported my commitment to feminist issues but understandably often, I think, wished I didn't bring my grievances into our home!]

The campaign to oppose ratification of the Equal Rights Amendment has been based, to a significant degree, on conscious deceptions and outright lies. Why has this been so?—Because the facts, honestly presented and fairly evaluated, overwhelmingly support the prompt passage of the Equal Rights Amendment to our federal constitution.

As the father of two young adult daughters; as the husband of a woman who has been fulltime homemaker, fulltime careerist, and a combination of both; as counselor to women, abandoned through divorce and struggling to survive with dignity as single parents or single persons: I know that women in the United States are unfairly discriminated against in education, in employment opportunities, in compensation for work done, and in legal status. No one who is informed can claim otherwise.

The Equal Rights Amendment is simple, clear, straightforward and fair. It has been repeatedly, unequivocally, overwhelmingly supported by the General Assemblies of the Unitarian Universalist Churches in North America for many years. It must become an integral part of the Constitution of the United States of America

—Minister's Column, **UU Congregation of Fort Wayne** *Newsletter*

Invitational Exhibit not Feminist Enough?

Unitarian Universalist Congregation of Fort Wayne
5310 Old Mill Road
Fort Wayne, IN 46807
Phone: 260–744–1867

July 21, 1981

Editor
The Journal Gazette
600 W. Main Street
Fort Wayne, IN 46802

Dear Editor:

The Invitational Exhibit '81 at the Fort Wayne Museum of Art, reviewed and selected by the internationally admired painter, Grace Hartigen, and hung under Julia Lyon's tasteful guidance, is a high quality show. Museum Director James Franklin and the museum's Board are to be congratulated on their perspicacity in sponsoring this display of works by members of the Indiana Women's Caucus for Art.

Was it ignorance, malice or both which prompted the review of this show by Robert Hertzberg in your July 12th edition? The purpose of the exhibit was to demonstrate that female artists work in all contemporary styles, media and subject matter with competence equal to that of male artists, and that there are no distinguishable characteristics of *female* art as distinct from *male* art. It was not to make a political statement of feminist convictions.

Responsible criticism of this show either would have produced examples of identifiable *female* characteristics evident in the show or would have claimed that the quality of the show overall is inferior to what a collection of all-male northern Indiana art would be. Neither is the case.

On what grounds did Hertzberg justify criticizing this show for not generating feminist political statements? I happen to know that some of the artists are, in fact, convinced and persuasive feminists who have used their talents and reputations extensively to support feminist causes for many years.

Thus, it is not for a lack of awareness, sensitivity or commitment that *feminist* themes do not predominate in this show. Rather, this exhibit serves a broader long-range vision. In its own well-defined terms it is a great success.

Thanks to the Fort Wayne Museum of Art for bringing it. I urge all who are interested in high-quality art to go see it.

—Yours truly, Rev Richard Langhinrichs

Rejuvenating Visions

As 1982 begins, I see us as standing in need of a fresh vision from religion. For a very long time now, religion has been functioning as a reactive, rather than a shaping, force: reactive, that is, in its responses to the discoveries of science; the complexities of technology; the incredible material riches of most Europeans, East Asians and North Americans; and the accompanying rise in population and gradual disappearance of natural resources such as oil, natural gas, pure water and uncontaminated air.

The so-called religious liberals have reacted by instituting novel liturgical nostrums; reluctantly revising prayer and hymn books while spawning a bewildering succession of theologies; repeatedly compromising with secular powers; and futilely—if not absurdly—expending much human energy on ill-conceived or peripheral objectives.

The so-called religious conservatives are equally unproductive. A thirteenth or a sixteenth or a nineteenth century ecclesiastical style (and they were all different) are irrelevant in today's world. Those who persist in sustaining one of them do so through the toleration of self-deception or, even more dangerously, of spiritual schizophrenia—the split-minded denial of reality.

A fresh perception of the Divine expectations of us and our limitations and potentialities both for good and for evil must be forged. While human cultures everywhere are floundering, religious insights are mostly superficially banal and/or dangerously nostalgic.

Our task in 1982 is to be open to rejuvenating visions and to resist as best we can all demonic temptations to shut our hearts and minds to them.

—Minister's Column, **UU Congregation of Fort Wayne** *Newsletter*

Minister-on-Loan in Texas

[**Editor's Note:** Dick's lodging in Amarillo, Texas was in the home of a member of that congregation, a prominent business man in the home security business. His home, where I stayed when I came to visit, was super-safe: one needed a code to punch in numbers to enter his home and, as I recall, similar codes to get into the various bedrooms, study and so on. (Dick had confided earlier that some members of this congregation wore lots of gold and fur…) Even so, I was not prepared, apparently, for a side trip we were planning. Our host listened patiently as we went over a map, and then broke in. He turned to Dick and asked, "Do you know how to use a pistol?"]

Carol VerWiebe (CV) Interviews Dick Langhinrichs (DL) about the Minister-on-Loan Program for church publication in the winter of 1983:

CV: *Why were you and our church selected for the Minister-on-Loan Program?*

DL: In the spring of 1979 the Unitarian Universalist Association was looking for a strong, effective, middle sized church to participate in the program. We voted to commit ourselves at that time.

CV: *Why are we just starting our participation now?*

DL: We aren't. There was an emergency in Indianapolis in the spring of 1979 and I spent two periods of three weeks each there helping to organize the Unitarian Universalist Church of Indianapolis. Since that time, each year we have again been asked to be part of the program.

CV: *For how long are you and the Fort Wayne Unitarian Congregation committed to the Minister-on-Loan Program?*

DL: Our commitment is open-ended. Some churches and ministers have participated three or four times. Both feel it is a very beneficial experience.

CV: *How were you and Amarillo matched up?*

DL: There were nine choices. Reverend Bill Holway, staff member of the denomination's Extension Office in Boston, made the matches last spring at the General Assembly in Vancouver. Actually, the Inter-District Representative from that area, Reverend Russell Lockwood, saw my name on the list and requested me.

CV: *How were the congregations selected?*

DL: The Extension Office chooses those congregations that they feel would most benefit. The Extension Office is charged with stabilizing the denomination and encouraging growth.

CV: *What will be our congregation's part in the Minister-on-Loan Program?*

DL: The congregation has already begun work. At a meeting on September 25th they had an opportunity for input about the proposed plans. I will be gone for six weeks. We have made a proposal to the Amarillo board that I will be there from February 1 to March 15. Our congregation will continue to pay my salary. That is our contribution. Amarillo will pay travel expenses, housing, car and secretarial costs. There are ongoing ministerial services that must be provided here: hospital and home calls, weddings, funerals. There must be six high-quality Sunday services. The office must continue to function smoothly.

CV: *Tell me a little bit about the Amarillo congregation.*

DL: The average pledge is $372. There are seventy-one adult members. There is not a strong religious education program or Sunday school. There is, however, a building seating one hundred that the congregation erected in 1969. And Amarillo is about the same size as Fort Wayne.

Wedding Celebrations

[**Editor's Note:** Both our daughters were married by Unitarian ministers in a Unitarian setting. Dick was frequently asked to perform weddings for the *unchurched,* as we called them. Although I was usually invited to the reception, if not the service as well, I attended only those of the church family. Why would I want to witness a ceremony at a bowling alley, a roller rink, or an empty train station? Nevertheless, some of those folks, Dick would point out, would eventually find their way to us. And they often did.]

Julie Langhinrichs and Benjamin Pease Lewis are planning a June 30 wedding in Philadelphia, Pennsylvania. Their parents are the Reverend Richard and Ms. Ruth Imler Langhinrichs, 459 Englewood Court, Fort Wayne, Indiana, and the Reverend David and Ms. Frances Lewis, East Aurora, New York.

The bride-elect is a graduate of South Side High School (1977), Swarthmore College (1981) and Lesley College, Cambridge, Massachusetts, where she obtained an M.ED. degree in 1982. She teaches at the Springside School for Girls, Chestnut Hill, Pennsylvania. Mr. Lewis is a graduate of the Park School of Buffalo, New York, and is a senior at Swarthmore College.

The couple will be married at the Unitarian Universalist Church of the Restoration, Gorgas Lane, Philadelphia. Their fathers will jointly officiate.

—Fort Wayne Journal Gazette, **June 11, 1984**

Julie Langhinrichs' wedding in 1984: included
the two minister fathers officiating the service
and the two mothers (not pictured) as ushers.

What Do You Think?

Fifty years ago this month as this church was about to be chartered, I enrolled as a freshman in the famous School of Speech of Northwestern University, Evanston, Illinois. A seventeen-year-old, I was an idealistic but far-from-innocent young man from a very wicked Mississippi River city. I immediately took up smoking unfiltered Camels, learned how to do heavy drinking, and without a second thought joined a fraternity in my first year. I wanted to pass as a blasé, smooth sophisticate as soon as possible, (especially because I was on a scholarship, worked for my room and board, and had about $3 a week in spending money). So with as much savoir-faire as I could muster, I played Gershwin's *Porgy and Bess* and *Rhapsody in Blue*, and learned to say *oh God* about almost everything.

Next Friday, the 317-member high school class of 1938 will gather in Rock Island, that once wicked river city. I'll be there. As depression kids, we were all decisively marked in various ways. We had experienced parental suicides, joblessness, house losses, droughts, and dust storms. We have remained remarkably faithful friends with each other throughout

World War II—almost all of the males were in it—and all that has since transpired. We know the fates and/or whereabouts of all 317 of us—a remarkable state of affairs.

I have sought during my life to remain idealistic despite my early and pretty complete loss of innocence about life and my pretensions to sophistication. In some small ways I have succeeded. Nevertheless, I have repeatedly been told that my involvement in idealistic causes have been impossible, worthless endeavors. All the facts are not yet in! What do you think?

—Rev. Richard Langhinrichs, September 8, 1988

Start-Up Minister in Indianapolis

[**Editor's Note:** Here the letter writer, a resident of Indianapolis, and a member of Dick's Start-Up Church there, is referring to a production of *A Morning with Gene Stratton Porter,* a program which Dick and I put together for the Sunday Service of a Fort Wayne week-end meeting of all the UU churches in the district. Not only did Dick support me in this, he also served as director, which involved the production of an audio tape that included the song of the cardinal!]

Dear Ruth,

Going through some desk drawers, I came across this program from 1981. I've often remembered the wonderful G.S.P [Gene Stratton-Porter] program (and the cookies and buttermilk refreshments). I would guess you have a copy of it, but just in case you don't, this one is yours.

That was such a fun morning. I think I'd just finished reading most of her books, so it was especially interesting to me. And I particularly enjoy cold buttermilk!

I have several of her books in my library. I'm getting along in years and am thinking who might benefit from them. In many ways she was ahead of her times, wasn't she?

I hope you're well and busy as you want to be. I'm ok for my age, I guess! My only child (59!) is moving from the Naperville, IL area to Eugene, Oregon this month. I'll certainly miss her. Eugene is so much farther than Naperville. I *may* follow her out there after a time. We'll see.

I'm sure you miss Dick as much as I miss Jim. I don't like being a widow.

Do you remember Linda Vaughn (wife of Larry V) at U.U.I.? She died a few months ago from multiple cancers. She was only fifty-seven.

I hope you have some pleasant reminisces from the program as I have.

Affectionately, Evelyn B, August 8, 2001

Former UUCFW Intern Appointed
Chief Immigration Judge

[Editor's Note: David Neal, a former UUCFW intern, was a junior high classmate of our daughter, Julia. Dick helped him with the paperwork to enter first Wabash College and then the Harvard Divinity School.

After serving a parish, David concluded he needed a law degree to anchor some of the necessary injustices he was witnessing. He went to Columbia University in New York City to do so. I visited him there and incidentally encountered, in the Ladies Restroom, Carolyn Kennedy, a law school classmate. Ever the eavesdropper, I chuckled to myself at a discussion of "how some women can get just too tan." As David's *Ma*, I immediately began to design a match, but David had another woman in mind.]

Falls Church, VA.—Executive Office for Immigration Review (EOIR) Director Kevin D. Rooney announced today that he has appointed David L. Neal as EOIR's Chief Immigration Judge. Prior to his appointment, Judge Neal had been acting in this capacity since April 2006. Before becoming Acting Chief Immigration Judge, Judge Neal served as an Assistant Chief Immigration Judge (ACIJ) from April 2005 to April 2006. He also served as an immigration judge at the Headquarters Immigration Court from June 2004 to April 2005.

Prior to his work within the Office of the Chief Immigration Judge, Judge Neal served as special counsel to the Director, EOIR, from January 2003 to June 2004. From October 2001 to January 2003, he served as chief counsel to the Senate Immigration Subcommittee. Judge Neal was an attorney advisor for the Board of Immigration Appeals (EOIR's appellate component) from November 1996 to October 2001.

Judge Neal practiced immigration law in Los Angeles from June 1993 to October 1996 and also served as the director of policy analysis for the American Immigration Lawyers Association from August 1990 to May 1993. He received a Bachelor of Arts degree in 1981 from Wabash College, a Master of Divinity degree in 1984 from Harvard Divinity School, and a Juris Doctorate in 1989 from Columbia Law School. He is a member of the New York and District of Columbia Bars.

The Chief Immigration Judge provides overall program direction, articulates policies and procedures, and establishes priorities for more than 200 Immigration Judges located in fifty-four Immigration Courts nationwide.

Immigration Judges are responsible for conducting formal administrative proceedings to determine whether foreign-born individuals who are charged with violating immigration law should be removed from the United States or may be granted relief from removal. Immigration judges decide each case independently, and their decisions are final unless appealed or certified to the Board of Immigration Appeals.

—News Release: Office of Legislative and Public Affairs, U.S. Dept. of Justice, Executive Office for Immigration Review, March 21, 2007

*Dick co-officiated David Neal's wedding
in Boston, Massachusetts*

A Beloved Community

[**Editor's Note:** A flame within a chalice (a cup with a stem and foot) is a primary symbol of the Unitarian Universalist faith tradition. Many of our congregations kindle a flaming chalice in gatherings and worships. Deutsch, an Austrian artist, first brought the chalice and flame as a UU symbol during his work with the Unitarian Service Committee during World War II. To Deutsch, the image had connotations of sacrifice and love. Today we have many different interpretations of the flaming chalice, including the light of reason, the warmth of community and the flame of hope.]

In 1959, I married a long-time college friend, Dick Langhinrichs, who significantly for the outcome of his courtship, had become a Unitarian Universalist in Detroit at the same time I had done the same, totally unknowingly and independently, in Philadelphia.

Three years after we were married and became the parents of two daughters, Dick had the dream of becoming a Unitarian Universalist minister; three years later, after graduating from the Harvard Divinity School, this congregation called him as its minister, his first and only ministry. Today our daughters and their families attend Unitarian Universalist churches in their areas.

I light the chalice this morning not only to celebrate the commitment of my family but the commitment of all those who strive to live the Unitarian Universalist principles, who engage themselves as well in creating and sustaining a Beloved Community, a community, where an individual can find strength, meaning and love. A community where, together the still incredibly pure in heart are capable of such a fierce courage that impossible dreams can—and do—come true.

—Ruth Imler Langhinrichs

Epilogue

Retirement Plans
Emeritus Proclamation
Review of Dick's Quest
Obituary
Memorial Service
Acknowledgments
Ahead of his Time
Forward Through the Ages
Announcing the 75th Anniversary of UUCFW
Benediction

Retirement Plans

In the last two-and-a-half years, we have often been overwhelmed by your generosity and your loving concern for our personal wellbeing, which reminds me of the 18th century quote by Henry Carey: "Our congratulations flow in streams unbounded." While our attention was usually so focused on surviving the multiple health crisis, we may have failed to communicate our heartfelt appreciation. Our *gratitude* flows beyond measure..

We hope you all understand that our infrequent attendance at Sunday worship is only due to our desire that your choice of our successors be the best ones possible. The UUA guidelines, advising retiring clergy persons to divorce themselves fully from all church business, are very wise. We fully subscribe to them. They are based on many years of experience.

After you have chosen and settled your new minister and ministerial family, we shall resume regular attendance at worship as part of expressing our unqualified support of the choice you make. In the meantime, we shall limit our involvement to being with you at social events, concerts, theatre; whatever.

Your generous monetary settlement on us when we retired last summer is deeply valued. Our May trip to Greece is, in part possible because of your ample gifts. We are grateful. We love all of you and know that you love us.

—Richard and Ruth Langhinrichs

*One of our Annual Retreats at the cottage of
David and Jackie Pietz in Rochester, Indiana*

Emeritus Proclamation

One score and four years ago our congregation ordained in this room a new minister, Richard Langhinrichs, conceived in liberality and dedicated to the proposition that all Unitarians are created equal.

Now we are engaged in a great period of change, testing whether this congregation, or any congregation so conceived and so dedicated can long endure. We are met in a great time and place. We have come to dedicate a portion of our love as a tribute to Richard, who gave a significant portion of his lifetime here that this congregation might live. It is altogether fitting and proper that we should do this.

But in a larger sense, we cannot dedicate—we cannot consecrate—we cannot hallow—this ground. This man, who struggled here, has consecrated it far above our poor power to add or detract. The world will little note nor long remember what we say here but Unitarians can never forget what he did here. It is for us, the congregation, rather, to be dedicated here to the unfinished work which he has thus far so nobly advanced. It is rather for us to be here dedicated to the great task remaining before us—that from this honored man we take increased devotion to the cause for which he gave full measure of devotion; that we here highly resolve that he shall not have labored in vain; that this congregation shall have a new birth into its second half century; and that this congregation of the people, by the people and for the people shall not perish from that portion of the earth known as Fort Wayne, Indiana.

And so, by the authority and privilege vested in me, I now bestow upon you the title of Minister Emeritus to the Unitarian Universalist Congregation of Fort Wayne. This designation is witnessed by your many friends in the congregation, both present and absent. May you enjoy it in great peace and much joy for a very long time. But even more importantly, may you enjoy and value it as a token of our collective enjoyment, our pride, our joy and our deepest appreciation for your service to this congregation.

It is the day-to-day accumulation of leaves and sticks, of branches and trees, gathered together in place and compressed in time that result in the diamond of our love for you, your ministry, your family, your very presence. This does not mean that I stand here to present you with a ten carat diamond, but rather that I stand to pledge our love, our adoration and our admiration to you for today, tomorrow and for always.

As rich as your service to us has been, so shall our love for you enrich your days, your memories... and our own.

E Anthony McNair, President (aka Abe Lincoln), 1989

Review of Dick's Quest

The ministry would become his career, but not until Richard (Dick) Alan Langhinrichs had been a struggling novelist, a successful real estate manager in New York's Greenwich Village and a highly paid business executive, managing 500 employees for Palace Quality Laundry/Dry Cleaners in Detroit, Michigan.

In search of a vocation which would offer more personal meaning, he entered the Harvard Divinity School at the age of forty-one, earned his S.T.B. in 1965 and accepted a call to Fort Wayne, Indiana, where he served the congregation for twenty-four years—until his retirement in 1989.

During this time, Langhinrichs emerged as a leader of social change in the conservative city of Fort Wayne, *a city of churches* in the northern tip of the Midwestern Bible Belt. He was chairman of the *Welcome Neighbor* integrated housing program in the 1960s, President of the Human Relations Council, and a member of the Citizens' Advisory Council when the Fort Wayne schools were partially integrated in 1971. He was a member of Citizens for Peace and the Draft Information Center during the Vietnam War and one of five Hoosier delegates to the Conference to End the War in Vietnam held in Paris, France, in 1971. He served as a founder, director and officer of the Northeast Indiana Planned Parenthood and Civil Liberties Union chapters. Langhinrichs helped organize a speakers' bureau to counter inflammatory public statements from the John Birch Society; and offered ground-breaking open support for gay and lesbian members of the community.

"Looking back on the decades he served here, it's hard to find an unpopular cause he didn't champion," observed the *Fort Wayne Journal Gazette* on the day following his death, July 31, 1990: "He mixed comfortably with business people and leaders of conservative bent, but it was usually to those who had no one to champion their cause that Langhinrichs was most strongly drawn."

After graduating cum laude from Northwestern University in the middle of World War II, he volunteered his services in the U. S. Marine Corps, where he served as a First Lieutenant and was awarded both the Bronze Star and Purple Heart for his participation in the battles of Tarawa, Saipan, Tinian and Okinawa. Langhinrichs, however, described himself as a peace activist.

"Non-violence has been a major concern of mine throughout my ministry," he said. "There has to be civil discourse between human beings or democracy cannot survive."

Although first and foremost a minister to his congregation, his public contribution grew out of his sense of ministry: in scholarship, education, participation in the democratic process and especially in the power of civil discourse.

Rev. Langhinrichs is listed in *Who's Who of the Midwest*, 22nd edition, 1990–91, and *Who's Who in the World*, 10th edition, 1991–92.

—Roberta Kreicker

*Dick Langhinrichs and Ruth with daughter Jenny
at her graduation from Brown University*

Obituary

The Rev. Richard A. Langhinrichs died in Fort Wayne, IN on July 31, 1990. He was 69 years old.

Born in Moline, IL, he excelled in oratory and acting as a student, and graduated from Northwestern University with a B.S. degree in speech in 1942. During the Second World War, he served as a first lieutenant in the Second Marine Division. He was awarded the Bronze Star for heroism in action at Saipan and the Purple Heart for battle wounds. Following the war, he worked in business until 1962, when he decided to study for the Unitarian Universalist ministry. In 1965, he graduated from Harvard Divinity School and accepted a call to the Unitarian Church of Fort Wayne, which he served continuously for 24 years until his retirement in 1989, when he was named Minister Emeritus.

The Rev. Langhinrichs was active in the community, as a founding member of local chapters of Planned Parenthood and the American Civil Liberties Union. His voice was raised in opposition to the Vietnam War and rightwing extremist groups.

He is survived by his wife, Ruth, of Fort Wayne, and two daughters.

[Nov/Dec 1990 Issue *The World*]

Memorial Service

Date: August 4, 1990

Speakers:
Rev. Charles Thomas (officiating)
Jenny Langhinrichs
Rev. Shermie Schafer (officiating)
Rev. Jerry Wright
Dianna Thornhill-Miller [Auld]
David Neal (officiating)

Rev. Charles Thomas:

Welcome. We are assembled as a family to celebrate the life of Richard Alan Langhinrichs. We gather for music, meditation, remembrance, and worship, but also to grieve together and share the burden of our sorrow. He remains in our hearts and his memory will continue to touch our lives, although he will no longer walk among us, or minister to our needs. Within his extended family here today, and his friends and colleagues across the country, he was called Dick, so that is how I will refer to him hereafter.

Dick was proud to be a Midwesterner. He loved this area of the country and left his mark on it. Dick lived longer in the house on Englewood Court than any other place, it was home. Dick loved Fort Wayne and made a real difference here. He spent twenty-four years serving this congregation in this meeting house where we have assembled today to share our personal memories of him. We're not going to list the details of Dick's life—that's been done by the local newspaper, which is reprinted in your inserts. Nor will we list his many services to the broader Unitarian Universalist movement. That too will be covered well by the various publications of our continental association. Rather, our remembrances will focus on those features which will not be available in printed form.

Dick and I have had many parallels in our lives. He was forty-one when he entered seminary; I was thirty-eight. He left a successful career in business; I was an engineer. Julie and Jenny are each slightly older than our two daughters. Neither Ruth nor Nancy, my wife, signed on to be a minister's wife, but both stuck it out. When I met Dick and saw what a minister could be, I was inspired to pursue a similar career. Dick's encouragement helped me find the courage to follow that dream, to answer that call and to survive the disappointments and setbacks.

Most of you here can tell a similar story and I encourage you to do so with Ruth throughout the coming weeks. David Neal and I were planning this memorial service with Ruth and her daughter Jenny last Thursday when the mail arrived. Ruth shared a couple of the cards with us and I'm going to share just one with you today. The card was from Joe Levine and his quote was from *Ethics of Fathers* by Rabbi Simeon: "There are three crowns for a man to wear: A crown of priesthood, a crown of royalty and a crown of Torah. But the crown of a good name excels all." This struck me hard at the moment when I first read it. It seemed to me it described Dick. He clearly qualified for all four crowns. With just a little modernization of the ancient text, let me describe how these crowns applied to Dick. First, the crown of priesthood: Dick was a spiritual leader in all of his communities, this congregation, this city and the continental association of Unitarian Universalists; Second, the crown of royalty: Dick never thought himself as royalty, but this can easily be modernized into administration. And Dick clearly had an administrative ministry in the many social and political causes that he championed. Third, the crown of Torah: it's easy to modernize that into learning or scholarship. Dick was both learned and scholarly.

Dick received many awards, much public recognition—crowns if you will—for his spiritual, administrative and scholarly skills. Still I will agree that his crown of a good name reigns supreme. My dissatisfaction came from the realization that at least in my presence Dick never identified himself with any of those words. Whenever Dick introduced himself it was as *minister*. Depending on a situation, he might add Unitarian Universalist of Fort Wayne or whatever else seemed appropriate.

But always he was a minister. At the risk of making this sound like an ordination service, I want to focus on one aspect of ministry that doesn't get emphasized often enough but that Dick's ministry highlighted for me. There is legend from the Torah. A rabbi came upon Elijah and asked, "When will the Messiah come?" Elijah replied, "Go and ask him yourself." "Where is he?" "Sitting at the gates of a city." "How shall I know him?" "He is sitting among the poor, covered with wounds. The others unbind their wounds all at the same time and then bind them up again. But he unbinds one at a time and binds it up again, saying to himself, perhaps I shall be needed. If so, I must be ready so as not to delay for a moment."

So it was with Dick's ministry. Yes, he had to look after himself and care for himself, but at the same time he was always prepared to look after others. Dick was always ready to help another: whether that was an individual or another cause. Dick shared fully in the human condition as he understood and experienced his own pain. He was able to offer his life experiences as a resource to others who suffered. It's not always necessary to expose the pain or the exact nature of the pain, just to expose the knowledge of the pain. Dick saw clearly painful things in the world, painful things in individuals, and painful things in himself. He was effective in helping ease pain in others because he knew it himself. And I think that helping ease pain was Dick's way of responding to the human condition. Making his own pain available as healing power for others did not lead to the kind of exhibitionism that we sometimes see in very famous TV preachers. And it never caused Dick to whine about what was going on in his life.

What Dick had was a willingness to see his own pain and his suffering and disappointments as naturally occurring in the deepest part of the human condition which we all share in unequal measure. Dick said once, loving yourself is highly overrated. Yes, accept yourself as you are, make whatever small improvements you can and get on with life.

A minister's task, and Dick did this in many ways, is to remind others that we are all human. We're all mortal and imperfect, but healing always starts with the recognition that your specific problem is just an example of the general human condition. Dick has helped me to see that we are each human and that disappointment, pain and suffering are therefore natural. We cannot know the future but these things we do know: individuals will continue to experience pain and will continue to suffer. Coming together to share our pain and our suffering, as we are today, moves us forward to that healing.

I'm going to close this portion of our service with a thought of Dick's: "The love that you can no longer give, give to someone else," followed by the Serenity Prayer:

> God grant me the serenity to accept the things I cannot change, the courage to change the things I can, and the wisdom to know the difference.

Jenny Langhinrichs:

I'm the youngest daughter in the family. I'm doing the first reading today and I'm going to read a poem by e. e. cummings, but before I do, I want to say a couple of things and it's probably going to be hard for me. But I'm going to try. First of all, some of you probably know me and a lot of you maybe don't. I'm standing here today alone, but actually I'm not really alone. I'm supported by my family, and by the church family, and they've been supporting us all week—very actively. And I'm supported by my mother and also my sister Julie, who I know is here with us in spirit. She couldn't be here today. Perhaps many of you know she's in Philadelphia recovering from childbirth. She had a little baby boy five hours after my dad died, and she named him Nathan Richard Langhinrichs. And she's with him and taking care of him right now.

But she's here too.

I suppose that many of you here today are thinking about my dad's intellect, his curiosity and creativity, his command of a vast breadth of knowledge, his high moral determination, his basically incessant fighting for a better world. And I want to say that I love those things about him, too. I do know, however, that it just wouldn't be right to say goodbye to him without just reminding all of you of his laugh. It was so loud, and so distinctive that I could pick him out of a darkened auditorium full of a thousand people. It actually happened once.

And I think too, it's really important to me to talk about his gourmet taste in food. We spent a lot of time as a family thinking about what to eat next. He was a man who always knew exactly what he wanted to eat. He'd be in the hospital and he'd say, I have to have a fried oyster sandwich, and we'd be out looking for one. And especially I guess his favorite foods were Tony's salami grinders or ravioli at Figaro's. And even the day before he died he was in the hospital at St. Joe's and he was going through menus trying to figure out what he wanted to eat, and circling butter and salt and it just wouldn't be right to say goodbye without thinking of him doing that.

And I guess the hardest of all for me to put into words is that I feel I need to say goodbye to Papa's struggle to overcome his obstacles, because he had his share to overcome. I really watched his body weaken. He had cancer ten years ago and it's been a really long struggle. But his spirit just kept fighting and fighting.

I think how he managed to keep going was that he always had a plan for the future, some goal he was working on or creative project, or something he wanted to learn about or a place he wanted to travel to. Maybe some of you know, six weeks ago, he was in Greece, traveling with my mother and Lillian. Less than a week ago he said to me, "I think I still want to go to New York and see some plays."

Most importantly to me, however, was the effort he made with me to keep learning about ways for him to try to love his family and to love me and my mom and Julie, and even maybe himself. He struggled with that a lot I think. And it seemed to me that every year that he stayed alive I got a little closer to him, and I felt a little clearer about how much love we shared between us. And for me it's really hard to say goodbye to that and to the opportunity to have more of that.

The excerpt of a poem that I'm going to read now is one that at some point in our lives everyone in our family has been at some library trying to find. We never knew the exact name of it, but it had to be there for Easter Sunday. It was part of his renewal celebration and I think it spoke to him about the necessity of really being alive when you're here. Its e. e.

cummings' poem *One Winter Afternoon* which ends with: "I thank heaven somebody's crazy enough to give me a daisy" which is why we always have daises on Easter Sunday, and why we will be giving you a daisy today.

From the poet Stephen Spender, we have an excerpt from *The Truly Great,* "I think continually of those who are truly great, who from the womb remember the soul's history."

And finally the 125th Psalm:

> They that trust in the Lord shall be as Mount Zion,
> Which cannot be removed, but abideth forever.
> As the mountains are round about Jerusalem,
> So the Lord is round about his people
> From henceforth, even for ever.
> For the rod of the wicked shall not rest
> Upon the lot of the righteous;
> Lest the righteous put forth their hands unto iniquity.
> Do good, O Lord, unto those that be good,
> And to them that are upright in their hearts.
> As for such as turn aside unto their crooked ways,
> The Lord shall lead them forth with
> the workers of iniquity:
> But peace shall be upon Israel.
>
> *[Psalm 125 KIV]*

Rev. Shermie Schafer:

Dick and I shared a love for the poetry of May Sarton, especially her poem *All Souls,* which begins, "Did someone say that there would be an end, an end, oh an end, to love and mourning?"

Dick also admired Marianne Moore and specifically requested that a reference to her poem *Nevertheless* be included. I selected the following words, "What is there like fortitude? What sap went through that little thread to make the cherry red?"

Early in his life Dick prided himself on his atheism. This poem from the *Spoon River Anthology* by Edgar Lee Masters is titled *The Village Atheist*:

Ye young debaters over the doctrine
Of the soul's immortality,
I who lie here was the village atheist,
Talkative, contentious, versed in the arguments
Of the infidels.
But through a long sickness
Coughing myself to death
I read the Upanishads and the poetry of Jesus,
And they lighted a torch of hope and intuition
And desire which the Shadow,
Leading me swiftly through the caverns of darkness,
Could not extinguish.
Listen to me, ye who live in the senses
And think through the senses only:
Immortality is not a gift.
Immortality is an achievement,
And only those who strive mightily
Shall possess it.

And this selection from *The Prophet* by Gibran on death:

Then Almytra spoke saying we would ask now of death. And he said, you would know the secret of death but how shall you find it unless you seek it in the heart of life. The owl whose night bound eyes are blind unto the day cannot unveil the mystery of light. If you would indeed behold the spirit of death, open your heart wide unto the body of life, for life and death are one even as the river and the sea are one. In the depth of your hopes and desires lies your silent knowledge of the beyond. And like seeds dreaming beneath the snow, your heart dreams of spring. Trust the dreams, for in them is hidden the gate to eternity.

Your fear of death is but the trembling of the shepherd when he stands before the king whose hand is to be laid upon him in honor. Is the shepherd not joyful beneath his trembling that he shall wear the mark of the King? Yet is he not more mindful of his trembling? What is it to die but to stand naked in the wind and to melt into the sun. And what is it to cease breathing but to free the breath from its restless tides that it may rise and expand and seek God unencumbered. Only when you drank from the river of silence shall you indeed sing. And when you have reached the mountain top then you shall begin to climb. And when the earth shall clean your limbs, then you shall truly dance.

Six years ago I was ordained into the Unitarian Universalist ministry and I asked Dick to deliver the charge to my ministry. And I'd like to share that with you. Dick said this in the charge based on the words of Dag Hammarskjold from *Markings*:

I don't know who or what put the question, I don't even know when it was put, I don't even remember answering, but at some moment I did answer yes to someone or something. And from that hour I was certain that existence is meaningful and that therefore, my life and self-surrender had a goal. From that moment I've known what it means not to look back and to take no thoughts for tomorrow. I came to a time and place where I realized that the way leads to triumph which is a catastrophe, and then to a catastrophe which is indeed a triumph. That the price for committing one's life would be reproach and that the only elevation possible to humans lies in the depths of humiliation.

And secondly, suggested by the words from Arthur Wakefield Slayten:

> We stand for a moment like those who pause upon a mountain pass and gaze downward to the valley and then look upward to the heights above which lower. We have been brought to our present point in part by powers we know not of, whether our feet shall even stand upon those high and lonely levels beyond depends upon us. We are like voyagers—when harbor dangers have been safely passed, the ship heads out to sea. From now on the voyage is our own. Ours is the task of making it a joy. Ours is to prepare the unfeeling, destructive storms, ours to find through comradeship with our fellows a sufficient inspiration.

And finally these words from Dag Hammarskjold: "In our era the road to holiness leads necessarily through the world of action."

And Dick's charge to me, as I think it would be to all of us was, first, commitment to your ideals. Secondly, to hold high your vision and finally, to be a person who through your actions demonstrates far more powerfully than words can say what it is to be a significant human being, an authentic human being in this day and age. May God bless *you*.

Rev Charles Thomas:

I invite you now to sing a song from the musical *Jacques Brell is Alive and Living in Paris*. One of the things I liked about Dick was that he was so in touch with what was going on all over the world, even in art and theater and drama and music, and these words to me exemplify so much of what Dick believed. You may not know the song, so we are sharing a tape from the sound track and I invite you to stand. If you'd like to just meditate upon the lyrics they are printed in the green insert in your program. Let's read together the first two lines, "If we only have love then tomorrow will dawn, and the days of our years will rise on that morn."

Rev. Jerry Wright:

I'm on the District Services Staff for the Unitarian Universalist Association but Dick Langhinrichs was *Mr. District*: A past president, a person with a sense of the interrelatedness of the congregations and need for administration and the importance of what it was all about anyway. Dick was in fact a member of the committee which invited me to take this position four years ago and he never let go of a sense of responsibility to make sure that things were going well. He was always asking, "How's it going?" and "How are they treating you?" I'm going to miss that a lot.

Dick was also a colleague. As ministers gather at least annually, one of the things we do is share our stories, our odysseys, as they are called. And a couple of years ago Dick shared his. I've heard many—his is the one I remember most. As we all do, he named and celebrated his accomplishments. But he went beyond that and with remarkable honesty named and celebrated the pain of his life and of his ministry. Named the pain he had caused others and the grief that brought him. It was a balance, a beautiful balance. My hope for myself is that someday when I am invited to give my odyssey, I might be blessed with the same courage and discernment to present a balanced picture. Not that I'm likely to accomplish a third of what Dick has accomplished. Only that I might present a balanced picture, that I might own the good stuff and the difficult times and to come to terms with both.

Dianna Thornhill-Miller [Auld]:

I've been asked to share some of my personal memories of Dick. And before I start I hope you'll forgive me, Jenny—I want to add to your recollections a memory that we shared yesterday. I think it's a good one for you to hear. Jenny was recounting some of the fun times and the laughter with Dick and the fact that he had the courage to do whatever he felt was appropriate in the situation. Jenny was a cheerleader, the Archer mascot, at South Side and South was in the Sectionals. And Dick showed up with green hair—cellophane. I know it was embarrassing at the time, but it's one of the things that she remembered and shared yesterday.

Dick has meant a lot of different things to each and every one of us. For me he was the model religious humanist. And at the same time he's immortal. I think because he touched so many of us in so many special ways that he'll go on and on. He taught us to recreate ourselves and our lives and our community and our world daily. His creativity is something which for me was very special, of course, as an artist. Other people have recounted the breadth of his intellect and his curiosity and his offerings to us that are so important and can't go unnamed. Jim and I came here twenty-one years ago. I was pregnant with our first son, and we were pilgrims looking for a place so that our children wouldn't grow up being dangled over the pits of hell, as we had been in our past traditional religious upbringing.

And we found Dick Langhinrichs here. He was a great teacher. Not a story teller but a great teacher. Somebody who was able to analyze and to fairly investigate—sometimes that was irritating to me—to have to listen to all the other sides, and to challenge us to grow and to act with commitment on our beliefs in this community and in the world. He was our representative in many ways. He did a lot of our reading for us. He was a personal friend that we could go to when we wanted to discuss things like where our children should go to college, personal choices—difficult and important decisions about our careers. Should we continue on this crazy experiment to create art, rather than earning money, for instance?

And his answer, of course, was, "yes." He encouraged us to follow our bliss, as Joseph Campbell did. He encouraged us by the examples of many of the great thinkers of all times in all the great religions. Reading from their sacred literature and up to current writers in politics and education, on peace, ecology, the arts and all of these ways he encouraged us, he challenged us, he provoked us and he inspired us to continue to give our gifts of art to the world. He continues I think to challenge us to create a new and better world in the future. Dick Langhinrichs is immortal.

David Neal:

I am a longtime friend and admirer of the Langhinrichs' family, and a former intern of this congregation. Several years ago, during a very painful period in my life, Dick and Ruth and their daughters, Jenny and Julie, took me into their home at a time when I really needed a home. What I found therein was a profound and wonderful family, fairly complex, and one that I must say is deeply committed to one another, struggling, wrestling with mutual love: a family that it's very easy to wish to be attached to. And over time I feel that I have because Dick was always *Pop* and Ruth has been *Ma* for a long time. I was fortunate enough to be able to observe Dick Langhinrichs in his many roles as father and husband, as minister, counselor, advocate and teacher.

However, when I sat down the other day and tried to think of what was most memorable about him I came across a particular instance at a summer retreat in which he was, as I recall, co-leading a lesson in Zen Buddhism. In the lesson, it was all about the art of dish washing. Where there is a special form where you hold the bowl reverently and you swish the water around in a certain way and you pay particular attention and detail to the very act of the washing. It is very important to be meticulous and very conscious of that washing. And as I recall, it was called "Doing the dishes to do the dishes." When I think about it, I think that was his secret.

For all his greater public skills, it was his mastery over the details that struck me as being his real strength and something that made him particularly special. He touched many lives through his ministry, but he touched many more through the day to day little things in which he remembered a name or a promise, a chore, even a laugh. There were those little things that struck me because the attention to detail that was very profound and I think it affected everyone around him. His whole consciousness of details made him able to treat each individual in a manner of respect and dignity that he believed all persons deserved.

I'd like to think of it as his way of doing the dishes. In the days and years to come when I think of him often and when the time comes that I think of him less, I will certainly remember him every time I do the dishes.

Rev. Charles Thomas:

In 1977, I was living just down the road in Richmond, Indiana and it so happened that both Dick and I totally unbeknownst to each other had signed up and agreed to go to Paris to find out why the Vietnam War peace talks were stalled. And we were greatly surprised to discover each other as the group assembled and so we glommed on to each other. I probably glommed more than he did—and we were roommates for that trip. Dick had taken high school French, and I had barely gotten through high school English. So he was a very handy fellow to be glommed with.

Those who are fluent in French said that Dick's French pronunciation was excellent—perhaps his attention to detail. But, his French grammar was clearly derived from the English. And one morning, we were in the hotel restaurant—the whole group ate together—and one of the ladies in the group wanted a hard-boiled egg. And she was like me, without French, and the waiter didn't have any idea what she was trying to say. And Dick wanted to rescue this lady and he struggled mightily to find in his French vocabulary what the French word for hard-boiled egg was. But it wasn't in his vocabulary. And finally, in his French he told the waiter that what she wanted was an egg to be boiled for five minutes. And the waiter got all excited and he said, "But, monsieur, it will get hard!"

Rev. Shermie Schafer:

I met both Ruth and Dick about the same time. Although I developed a warm friendship with them as a couple, I also had a unique relationship with just Dick and a unique friendship with just Ruth. Not many couples are able to do that. That was one of their gifts to me.

One of my earliest memories and meetings with Dick was as a ministerial student. I was just beginning my journey into a midlife career as a minister. But Dick never treated me as a student—it was always as a colleague. Our friendship developed later.

There are some humorous journeys that we shared literally as well as figuratively. I remember going to General Assembly in 1982 and the three of us poured ourselves into a car and drove non-stop to Brunswick, Maine, rotating drivers along the way.

We stayed in a cottage on Birch Island which had fourteen cottages and no electricity, where we shared our naiveté with mechanical toilets, solar showers, and gasoline lanterns that hung on the walls. Dick and

Ruth forgot that as dusk comes so does all life on the island, the first day they attended General Assembly. I had stayed by myself in our cottage, and was sound asleep when I heard a loud crash in the middle of the night, then sounds of fumble, fumble, fumble. A fog had rolled in and all the natives on the island had gone to bed early, so there were no lights to guide Ruth and Dick back to the cabin. They blindly stumbled along the beach and were cautiously fumbling their way back—with great restraint not to swear.

So far, my ministry has been in specialized ministries of chaplaincy and counseling. But every once in a while Ruth and I would be in the midst of a conversation and she would say, "You know, Dick would really like to see you take a parish sometime again." So there was that kind of gentle nudging for me to reclaim that part of my ministry. And ironically this summer such an invitation came. And a month from now, when I preach my first sermon in the Muncie, Indiana congregation, I will dedicate that day to Dick. And know that he would be pleased.

I think I could sum up Dick in one word—or what he offered as that word. It was his *hospitality,* which has been mentioned recently in the editorials and the printed reflections on his life. Dick lived out that hospitality not only on a global level, a corporate level, a community level but also in his home. And he assured me many times in the last year that not only was I welcome but my dog Sophie, who I recently adopted as a pup. Someone said to me recently: "You've heard of the child within. Well, German shepherd puppies are the child without." That's how Sophie was. But last Christmas she came into Dick and Ruth's home and rather than bounding from room to room, she very quietly settled down at the edge of the green chair in which Dick sat and fell asleep next to the fire with her nose across his feet.

I last saw Dick two weeks ago. I had attended a retreat with some of the members of this congregation and even in the midst of his obvious pain, his first words were, "So, how did it go?" And I expect I will hear that message again and again in my memory in the years to come.

I'd like to close my reflections with these words by May Sarton, written as a celebration for her father, and Jenny—this is for you and Julie, "I never saw my father old…He went out while the tide was full, still undiminished, and bountiful: a scholar and a gentle soul."

Rev. Charles Thomas:

We will close by singing the hymn *Forward Through the Ages*. As we sing, we will make a circle, and hold hands. Those of you in the narthex could loop into the room, and go back and forth around the rows. We'll sing until the circle is closed, then say the *World Peace Prayer* in unison. Ruth will then hug the person next to her—and the hug will be passed around the circle until it returns to her.

> Forward through the ages, in unbroken line,
> Move the faithful spirits at the call Divine;
> Gifts in differing measure, Hearts of one accord,
> Manifold the service, one the sure reward.

> **Chorus:**
> Forward through the ages, in unbroken line,
> Move the faithful spirits at the call Divine.

> Wilder grows the kingdom, reign of love and light;
> For it we must labor, till our faith is sight.
> Prophets have proclaimed it, martyrs testified,
> Poets sung its glory, heroes for it died.

> Not alone we conquer, not alone we fall;
> In each loss or triumph, lose or triumph all.
> Bound by God's far purpose in one living whole,
> Move we on together, to the shining goal.

> **Benediction:**
> Lead us from death to life, from falsehood to truth,
> Lead us from despair to hope, from fear to trust,
> Lead us from hate to love, from war to peace,
> Let peace fill our hearts, our world, our universe.

> —World Peace Prayer

Please take a daisy with you as you leave the sanctuary.

[**Editor's Note**: Excerpts of poems and lyrics (read in full during Dick's Memorial Service) were published herewith in accordance with copyright guidelines—which greatly diminished their sizes and intended emotional impact. However, it is possible to access some or all of them on the internet to read or purchase in their entirety, if you so desire. Those poems and lyrics are:

One Winter Afternoon, poem by e. e. cummings
The Truly Great, poem by Stephen Spender
All Souls, poem by May Sarton
Nevertheless, poem by Marianne Moore
If We Only Have Love, from the musical
Jacques Brell Is Alive and Living in Paris
A Celebration for George Sarton by May Sarton]

Rev. Shermie Schafer with Dick and Ruth
at another ceremony in honor of Dick

Acknowledgments

The magnitude of Dick's gift is so great that it has taken many hearts, minds and hands to represent it here:

The Langhinrichs family has bestowed their trust, support and vote of confidence in me. Their gift of challenge and opportunity for *The Great Yes* (changed to *Atheist in a Foxhole* in 2012) has been a privilege I shall always treasure.

Ruth Imler Langhinrichs is a former editor of four national publications: *Look, Scholastic, Science Illustrated* and *The Ladies' Home Journal.* She is a keen editor who improved the clarity and brevity of my original draft.

I owe a sincere *thank you* also to **Julie Langhinrichs**, the older Langhinrichs daughter, and **Jenny Langhinrichsen**, the younger daughter, who sent several delightful letters full of fond remembrances of "Papa."

Dr. James Luther Adams, Professor Emeritus, Christian Ethics, Harvard Divinity School. The Langhinrichs Family and I deeply appreciate Dr. Adams' valuable participation.

I am especially grateful to **Charles Heinemann, M.D.**, a local psychiatrist and my mentor, who gave me much insightful guidance from the start, helping to set and steady my course with key questions and much-respected suggestions. Danke!

Graham H Kreicker, Chicago advertising executive and former President of the Fort Wayne (Indiana) Congregation. In 1980, when Graham moved out-of-state, he arranged with the congregation's president to tape record RAL's sermons, which was followed by the inspiration to compile this book of RAL's sermons.

Tony McNair was the congregational president who meticulously recorded RAL's service every Sunday beginning in 1980. He would send tapes to Graham, who would record a copy and then send them on to The Rev. Charles Wilson in Marblehead, Massachusetts.

Rev. Wilson would record duplicates for his tape library, and then return them to Tony, who carefully maintained the tapes on file, all safely intact after their own spiritual journey from Indiana to Illinois to Massachusetts!

Mike Biesiada, Historical Records Committee— supplied 25 years' of RAL's more than 1,000 sermon files, made photocopies and ran errands.

Daniel Clark, research assistant, helped sort through the 1,000 sermon files to find topics selected by the editor and spent hours at the Historical Records office seeking answers to specific questions. Daniel, a college junior, spent his summer vacation giving this project a big boost.

Vickie Dohner, research assistant, has a masters degree in Social Work and is truly a hot-shot researcher. Vickie located many of the details inserted after a quotation source [nationality, profession, dates lived] as well as definitions for the manuscript's unfamiliar terms.

This project was research-intensive. The research team, **Daniel, Vickie and I,** were always on the trail for clarification, detail and verification. Fortunately, we had wonderful local resources and the capability for outreach beyond our own small region. It was an enriching endeavor and a most rewarding quest!

First, a grateful nod to the **Allen County Public Library** Readers' Services, the Business and Technology Department and the Music Department. The librarians are so superb that all I had to do was pick up the phone and ask!

Indiana-Purdue University at Fort Wayne (IPFW) was also highly professional and a wonderful resource. IPFW provided hard-to-find detail from several departments: the IPFW Library Reference Desk, **Professor Michael Downs** of the History Department; **Dr. Chowdhury** of the Geo-Space Sciences Department, several faculty and staff members of the Philosophy Department; and a professor, (whose name I failed to get), in the Economics Department for information on Arnold Toynbee.

Also, here in Fort Wayne, we called **St. Francis College** in search of **Father Noel Mailloux's** nationality and dates he lived. The **Rev. Margaret McCray-Worrall** advised this editor of the recent publication of

The Pastoral Care Encyclopedia which is how we located Father Mailloux. She readily answered several questions, as well.

Rabbi Richard Safran, of the Achduth Veshalom Temple, was a personal friend of Dick's. He graciously granted me an interview and helped reconstruct Dick's message on the benefits of diversity.

The **Harvard Divinity School Library** was amazing! The librarian was outstanding, which she just shrugged off as *just a little library detective work.*

The **Rev. Laurie Proctor** answered many questions and suggested a number of valuable resources.

Alan Seaburg, Andover-Harvard Library, sent resource information on the Spiral Galaxy symbol and on the Charles Street Meetinghouse (Boston) which was established by Kenneth L. Patton.

Elisabeth Hoffman, and the **Rev. Paul L'Herrou** of Boca Raton, Florida, provided information on the Interdependent Web.

President William Schulz made his President's Report in the September-October 1991 issue of the *Unitarian Universalist World* which was a primary component of our *Publication Proposal Packet and Grant Application.*

Julie Herman, Indiana University-Purdue University at Fort Wayne, media specialist in the News Bureau and Publications Department, and **Doug Ulmer,** attorney, researched and forwarded copies of the Fair Use Clause, establishing our exemption from the need for reprint permissions on some copyrighted material.

Kristi C. Heesch, UUA [Boston] sent an illustration of the Interdependent Web, and supplied considerable historical information.

With researchers like these, it was fairly easy to identify every quotation source and to clarify definitions of some terms and details. [Dick was truly an educated and literate man; it was indeed a learning experience and privilege to package his messages.]

Sue Fields, Fort Wayne (Indiana) UU secretary, fielded many questions, efficiently handled all our scheduling requests, made good referrals, and saw that our publicity releases were published in the earliest edition possible in *The UUnique Nuus* [Fort Wayne UU Congregation's newsletter].

Doug Powers, attorney, participated in core team early planning sessions, volunteered to do computer scanning and editing, and recruited a tape transcriptionist and an assistant for computer scanning and editing, and personally supervised the pre-press disk preparations.

Susan Sanford, legal secretary, transcribed Langhinrichs' sermon tapes.

Bonnie Caudill, legal secretary, assisted with computer scanning and editing, and downloaded the manuscript to disks for the printer.

Mary Jane Shearer, typographer, assisted with word processing and pre-press preparation. Her masters degree in typography and printing design enabled much refinement in our techniques!

The Fort Wayne downtown branch of **Instant Copy** processed *reams* of photocopied manuscript content, as did **Mike Biesiada** and **Doug Powers.**

Harriet Ulmer, an elementary school teacher, was one of our edit review readers. Her experience in evaluating and reporting on written work was quite beneficial.

Sharon and Bruce Mercer contributed a photo of Rev. Langhinrichs in full robes, sitting with an open Bible, near what appears to be a sundial. The Mercer wedding was Renaissance-style with the wedding party and the guests in period dress.

Lew Weber, a Marine sergeant in the Battle of Saipan, also served with Lt. Langhinrichs on several other battlefields. Lew loaned us some very valuable photos from Saipan which he took right after the Marines seized the island.

E. L. Fritz "Gene" was a Marine corporal who served under Lt. Langhinrichs' command during the invasion of Saipan in World War II's South Pacific. Fritz was the last person to talk with Lt. Langhinrichs from a Landing Ship Tank (LST) just prior to that invasion.

Ann Wintrobe contributed an interview form completed by Langhinrichs regarding his choice of *South Wind* by Norman Douglas as the most significant book he ever read. Read Dick's response in his list of books: *Sacred* Texts at the end of Part I.

The following additional persons also contributed their remembrances of Dick; they are greatly appreciated:

Mark S. Auburn
Michael T. Biesiada
Ina Dormire
David Fairchild
E. L. "Gene" Fritz
Nan Getzin
Rev. William Hammond
Rev. Ralph Helverson
Ezra C. Hill
Elaine Kirchner
Bruce Lakin
Ann McKenna
Dianna Thornhill Miller [Auld]
Dr. David and Jackie Pietz
Charles B. Redd
Rev. Shermie Schafer
Nagin Shah
Rev. Charles Thomas
Lew E. Weber
Rev. Charles L. Wilson
Caryl & Bruce Barton
E. David DeVoe
Nancy W. Doughty
Dean L. Frantz
Vish Gurundutt
Rev. Diana Heath
Rev. Kathleen Hepler
John J. Irwin
Graham H. Kreicker
Bruce and Sharon Mercer
David L. Neal
David C. Pohl
Rabbi Richard B. Safran

Rev. William F. Schulz
Gloria Still
Sushil K. Usman
Charles Franklin Willer
Ann Wintrobe

Much as musicians acknowledge their instruments after a pleasurable performance, I give an appreciative nod to my alter ego, *Gabby*—otherwise known as a word processor—for constancy, reliability and for the joy of it all.

And to Dick, who remains in all our hearts and minds, my heartfelt gratitude for the personal enrichment and spiritual growth I gained from this project.

Ultimately, I am deeply grateful for all your responses!

—Roberta Kreicker, 1992

Postscript: I feel honored to have completed what so many people who loved Dick and his family started back in 1992. I attended services in Fort Wayne with my five children and two grandchildren from 1962 until July 1970, at which time I moved to Dayton, Ohio where I became a member of First Unitarian Church for over twenty years. I returned to the UUCFW in 2000.

My contribution to this effort was minimal compared to the work that came before, but I feel privileged to have pushed it over the finish line.

—Betty Casbeer Carroll, 2015

Ahead of his Time

[**Editor's Note**: I recently received a note from Carol VerWeibe (a former member who moved to Bloomington, Indiana to be near her grandchildren after her husband Dick died in 2011), which came with a forty-year-old clipping.

This is the content of her note of July 1, 2014:]

Dear Ruth,

Do you remember Dennis and Rhea Mason? They were members of the church in the 1970s. (Dennis worked at Bowmar.) Dick and I remained close to them through the years.

The Masons are preparing to move to a retirement community (in Indianapolis) and are sorting through their possessions. They ran across the enclosed news clipping (from the Fort Wayne Journal Gazette) and sent it to me, which I am passing it on to you—it looks like (your) Dick was ahead of his time. —Love, Carol

The forty-year-old clipping, *Understanding is their Goal,* dated July 15, 1974 follows:

Because of acute misunderstanding about homosexuality, four people in Fort Wayne, Charlotte Salinger, John Escosa, Richard Langhinrichs and Larry Burke, appeared on a panel Sunday to discuss the formation of *Integroup,* individuals concerned in developing an understanding and to deepen the awareness of problems of persons who are homosexuals.

"We hope to provide counseling and to relate to the homosexuals about his or her problems," Richard Langhinrichs, a Unitarian minister, said. "It is an appropriate and much needed thing for Christians and religious people to do." The idea for Integroup grew out of Langhinrichs experiences with a similar group while he acted as a minister in a Unitarian Church in London, "I traded churches for six months with Keith Gilley, the English minister, who came to Fort Wayne and ministered at this church. Keith had been involved with the same thing in London, so I took over his duties while he was here. Though Integroup is not a formal act of the Unitarian Universalist Church, we are providing the place to meet and anyone may attend, though he or she may not be a member of our church. The four people involved on the panel have all had varying interests in homosexuality. Charlotte Salinger, a psychiatric social worker, has encountered problems in years of practice. There is confusion for adolescents who find themselves attracted to persons of the same sex and the social difficulties this can create. My job is the religious understanding involved. Religious view in the past have been simplistic: it's a sin, but if you exercise willpower, the problem will go away. Well, it isn't a sin, nor is that what the Bible says. Nor are we promoting or encouraging homosexuality. We just don't believe it's a contagious disease. Our group hopes to sponsor programs for persons and parents concerned in this area. Many people have a raft of misinformation and don't know where to turn. We would also like to sponsor social events for members and interested persons. Our purpose is that of helping people get to know one another."

Larry Burke is an attorney in Fort Wayne. As a member of the Unitarian church here, he was asked to head the legal portion of the panel. He stated that he is not an expert in the problems homosexuals have, and only knows what he's been told by others and what he has guessed at. He further said, "In the past, homosexuals have been prosecuted for violating the sodomy laws, and to my knowledge, that has been the legal focus of interest. We'd like to work to get the sodomy laws changed, since they are very simple and not too clear. Besides, if Kinsey is correct, sodomy is committed routinely by married couples as well as homosexuals. I was asked to draw up the bylaws, which are for an unincorporated group, with small dues for refreshments and mailing only. It's not planned that Integroup be a large lobbying group, but primarily a social thing. It's a chance for homosexuals and heterosexuals to get acquainted. In the past, heterosexuals have had a reservoir of fear and distrust, which is a cultural carryover of taboos. Males in particular feel threatened when they see what they consider to be *unmanly conduct*. We hope heterosexuals will become more comfortable with homosexuals, who have existed for centuries. Homosexuality is no longer considered a serious psychological disorder, but sexual activity by a homosexual is considered a felon. I'm more interested as a father and a person who has taught courses on sexuality."

—Journal Gazette, by Charlene Wilson, staff writer, July 15, 1974

Forward Through the Ages

The original title for this book, the working title, was *The Strength to Say Yes*—the title of Dick's first sermon delivered to the congregation of First Parish in Cambridge, Massachusetts where he was a student at the Harvard Divinity School. However, after we assessed the scope of the materials to be included, we realized that title wasn't adequate either. Perhaps, we wondered, if *The Great Yes* might be more appropriate.

As the book progressed, however, we realized even this title did not reflect all the attributes of the developing manuscript. This book is more than an account of a twenty-two-year-old Marine, an idealistic *atheist* who never stopped creating and protecting goodness, as well as fighting evil, in all its forms. This book, after all, is also about foxholes, those *temporary* shelters we hastily dig to provide some defense during an active battle within ourselves or those raging around us. (When asked what he believed, Dick's usual response was "Why are you asking?" or "I'm a mystic.") And the new working title became simply "Dick's Book."

In the inevitable word-to-word proofing of the manuscript, it also became apparent that the tone of Dick's *sermons* was informal, almost conversational, never dogmatic— usually a speculative and erudite thinking out loud. Consequently, we wanted the descriptive words *reflections and insights* somewhere on the cover.

Since this project began, other changes took place in the UU Meetinghouse and in our family. For instance, no one smokes in the meetinghouse anymore, but we drink wine on special occasions; there's carpet in the Sanctuary and the Social Hall, new upholstered chairs, a landscaped Memorial Garden with blooming rose bushes and a bubbling fountain. There's an addition to the building—a Religious Education wing with its own restrooms. Julie married Ben Lewis who changed his name to Langhinrichs as a wedding gift to Dick. They became the parents of Sara, Nathan and Matthew. Jenny married Martin (Marty) Rohling and changed her name to Langhinrichsen-Rohling. They became the parents of Ali, Roslyn and Ryan.

New names, too, now must be added to the list of the many, many individuals who contributed to this project: **Kirsten Eckert-Smith, Sandra Maze, Jan St. Clair, Jeanne Neuchterlein, Reverend Misty-Dawn Shelly**, our present minister, her spouse **Jenna Gervasi-Shelly** and **Betty Casbeer Carroll.**

I am especially appreciative of the encouragement of Reverend Misty-Dawn Shelly who welcomed this project and envisioned it of value in the celebration of the 75th Anniversary of the Unitarian Universalist Congregation of Fort Wayne (UUCFW). This gave us an unavoidable but dreaded deadline: the year 2014!

Jenna Gervasi-Shelly who volunteered to serve as proofreader/copy editor proved to be a pro at the job. For instance, she tracked down the exact version of the Bible being quoted (there were four different versions)—and made any additions, corrections or notations in beautifully, clear, legible handwriting! Furthermore, she was serene, diplomatic and cheerful throughout our nearly weekly meetings during that brutal winter and muggy spring: a treasured and good new friend [one minister's wife to another].

There would be no book if Betty Casbeer Carroll had not insisted (demanded?!) that we sit down and go through all the work that Bobbie Kreiker had done earlier (Part I) and other related materials and *get going*. Betty had published several books and said it not only could be done, it should be done. She gave me deadlines to collect photos (we were only allowed 25); she digitalized the typed manuscripts, letters, news clippings; she cut-and-pasted, added and deleted, made a fresh copy; she acted as liaison with the publisher. But best of all, she came up with the title for the book!

Although the three associate editors never worked together, each one contributed her own strengths and all three have in common a passionate commitment to perpetuating the message of this book.

––Ruth Imler Langhinrichs, 2015

Announcing the 75th Anniversary of UUCFW

On April 16, 1939, the Unitarian Meetinghouse was formally organized. Seventy-five years ago, the founders of our congregation gathered in rented quarters at the Fort Wayne Art School and at Fairfield Manor until 1945, when they purchased 2929 Fairfield Avenue for their first home of their own. In 1957, the congregation of 180 members voted to move forward with a new building and broke ground in June of 1960, here on Old Mill Road.

We have a rich history of Unitarian and Unitarian Universalist ministry here in Fort Wayne. As your ninth settled minister, I am privileged to continue the ministry that has served as a liberal religious voice in a religiously conservative community. The ministries of Robert Hoagland (1939–45), Aron Gilmartin (45–52), John Fordon (52–55), Hugo Leaming (56–61), Eugene Luening (61–65), Richard Langhinrichs (65–89),Laurie Proctor (91–2003) and Jay Abernathy (2004–10), have laid the stepping stones that have filled our faith community with growth in numbers, experience and service. In addition, the interim ministries and consultations of Gregg Carter, Michael Spath and Jennie Barrington have led to guidance and support as this congregation discerned its next steps in being a liberal spiritual sanctuary where all are welcome regardless of religious background, age, race, ethnicity, ability, gender and sexual orientation. As you and I journey together in shared ministry, we will continue the path with new stepping stones, twists and curves, always rooted in our heritage and with wings to soar (thanks to the hyperbolic parabloid roof!).

In the coming year, as we celebrate our 75th Anniversary with fun and fellowship, music and spoken word, coffee and champagne, we will have opportunities to remember our history and imagine our future. Be sure to connect with Laurie Proctor, our Minister Emerita, and me with your ideas, time and talent to make this a grand year of celebration of 75 years of Unitarian Universalism here in Fort Wayne!

May you let your light shine today, in the coming year, and for another 75 years or more!

Blessings, Rev. Misty-Dawn Shelly, 2014

Benediction

In the selection and emphasis we have given to the contents of this book, we have tried to draw a portrait of the depth, breath and complexity of a man whose quest for meaning led to a midlife career decision of enormous impact on his personal lifestyle and the wider community he lived in. As he so valiantly tried to meet the expectations of his calling and those of his personhood as a husband, father, brother, son, uncle and friend, he was in and out of more than one foxhole, just like the rest of us, only maybe with more remorse. He was a very human being.

Although all the facts by their very nature will never be in, dear Dick, your journey and legacy, I truly believe, will inspire generations to come, especially our own, I hope.

—With love, Ruth

Printed in the United States
By Bookmasters